"What an excellent resource! Here is a call to prayer that understands the prophetic, a call to intercession that understands the importance of Israel, a call to supplication that understands the Spirit. James Goll is one of the few leaders in the Body today who could write such a book, let alone do it with passion, biblical grounding and balance. This is highly recommended reading."

—Dr. Michael L. Brown, founder and president,
ICN Ministries

"I personally can attest to the intercessory grace on James Goll's life and his passion for Jesus, because I have walked with James for the past fifteen years. *The Prophetic Intercessor* will add needed ammunition to the prayer arsenal to inspire effective, fervent prayer from the heart."

—Mike Bickle, ministry director, Friends of the Bridegroom;
International House of Prayer

"James Goll has done it again! Few can put it together like him in concept and application. Touch this work and you will be touched."

—Jack Taylor, president, Dimension Ministries

"James Goll is a man God has used to give my life prophetic direction and definition. James is sold out to God. He has been used to bring healing and encouragement to me and the church I lead in Iowa."

—Francis Frangipane, River of Life Ministries

"In this intensive study of the Bible, James Goll has uncovered a host of ways people prayed that worked. If one method failed to get the desired answer, God would lead them to a new level, using a different approach. Learn from the mighty heroes of faith—as James introduces them to us—both from the Bible and from history, those who moved God for great miracles.

"This volume could and should revolutionize your own life as you discover and put to use the means God has provided to answer your own prayers. If you are a minister, a teacher, a leader, a parent, share this exciting revelation of praying prayers that work. This is a timely, much-needed book, as God looks for and no doubt wonders where the intercessors are (Isaiah 59:16). It's high time for the world changers to arise as the nations move into uncertain waters. God has the answer!"

—Freda Lindsay, chairman of the board emeritus,
Christ for the Nations, Inc.

"If the Lord eternally titled His own house as a 'House of Prayer,' there must be incredible depths and dimensions of prayer we have yet to discover. One who could show us such profound and prophetic revelation would need to be a humble seeker, a desperate travailer and a warring prevailer. I know of no man more qualified to take us on that journey than James Goll."

—Dr. Ché Ahn, senior pastor, Harvest Rock Church

"Not only does James Goll have an excellent prayer and prophetic ministry; he also has an ability to teach and equip the Body of Christ with excellence."

—John Arnott, senior pastor, Toronto Airport Christian Fellowship

"I have a prescription for every believer who needs vitality in his or her prayer life. Devour this book! For those who want to intercede for family, friends and the nation, James Goll gives a blueprint for action in the Spirit realm. It places within your hands God's battle plan for victory. James gives not just an understanding of the theology of intercession but how the principles apply in your daily life.

"I remember well the testimony of healing from barrenness that this book vividly describes, because I was used by the Lord as a tool of mercy in the Master's hands. As a result, not only do the Golls have four children today, but James and Michal Ann have entered into a depth of prayer and are able to impart these truths to the lives of believers. I encourage every believer in every church to allow the Holy Spirit to weave the great truths contained in *The Prophetic Intercessor* into the fabric of their lives."

—Mahesh Chavda, founder and senior pastor,
All Nations Church, Charlotte, North Carolina

"The last thing the Body of Christ needs is another gimmicky book on prayer. James Goll hasn't given us one. Instead, he speaks of the kind of biblically informed intercession that transformed the age of Wesley, set ablaze the meadows of Cain Ridge and, as in Wales and Zambia, shaped the course of nations. If it is true, as Jonathan Edwards said, that 'when God determines to give His people revival, He sets them a-praying,' then this book is as much a hopeful sign as it is a fresh unveiling of God's ways."

—Stephen Mansfield, founder, The Mansfield Group

THE
PROPHETIC
INTERCESSOR

THE
PROPHETIC
INTERCESSOR

Releasing God's Purposes
to Change Lives
and Influence Nations

Revised Edition

JAMES W. GOLL

Chosen
Grand Rapids, Michigan

© 1999, 2007 by James W. Goll

Published by Chosen Books
A division of Baker Publishing Group
P.O. Box 6287, Grand Rapids, MI 49516-6287
www.chosenbooks.com

Revised and updated edition of *Kneeling on the Promises*

Second printing, August 2007

Printed in the United States of America

Library of Congress Cataloging-in-Publication Data

Goll, Jim W.
      The prophetic intercessor : releasing God's purposes to change lives and influence nations / James W. Goll.
            p.   cm.
      Rev. ed. of : Kneeling on the promises.
      Includes bibliographical references (p.   ) and index.
      ISBN 10: 0-8007-9417-6 (pbk.)
      ISBN 978-0-8007-9417-0 (pbk.)
      1. Intercessory prayer—Christianity. I. Goll, Jim W. Kneeling on the promises.
II. Title.
BV215.G65 2007
248.3′2—dc22   2006034302

Unless otherwise indicated, Scripture is taken from the New American Standard Bible®, Copyright © 1960, 1962, 1963, 1968, 1971, 1972, 1973, 1975, 1977, 1995 by The Lockman Foundation. Used by permission.

Scripture marked AMPLIFIED is taken from the Amplified® Bible, Copyright © 1954, 1958, 1962, 1964, 1965, 1987 by The Lockman Foundation. Used by permission.

Scripture marked TLB is taken from *The Living Bible*, copyright © 1971. Used by permission of Tyndale House Publishers, Inc., Wheaton, Illinois 60189. All rights reserved.

Scripture marked NIV is taken from the HOLY BIBLE, NEW INTERNATIONAL VERSION®. NIV®. Copyright © 1973, 1978, 1984 by International Bible Society. Used by permission of Zondervan. All rights reserved.

Scripture marked NKJV is taken from the New King James Version. Copyright © 1982 by Thomas Nelson, Inc. Used by permission. All rights reserved.

Scripture marked KJV is taken from the King James Version of the Bible.

This book is dedicated to my dear wife of more than thirty years, Michal Ann Goll.

You are an example of character and gifting brought together in one unique combination! Thanks for being a fighter and helping to pave the way for a generation of prophetic intercessors to arise. You are my best friend and greatest support in life and ministry. I love and need you.

James W. Goll

Contents

CONTENTS

Foreword

THIS MORNING I arose early and went into my prayer room. There is a little, old-fashioned couch in a corner of the room that is my "kneeling spot." Each day when I am at home in Texas, like I used to do when we lived in Colorado, I like to rise early and meet God in that quiet place. From that small spot on the floor I travel around the world praying, doing exactly what James Goll describes in this book. I am aware, however, that I am not alone in my travels in prayer. All over the world, voices are joining mine in many languages—the harmony of God's children calling out to Him in intercession.

This prayer movement has grown throughout the 1980s and '90s and has now mushroomed in the 21st century. Whereas many churches did not have prayer rooms and ministries when we started teaching on intercession, there are numerous ones today. In fact, today, entire nations have prayer networks made up of radical, prophetic intercessors. That is why this book, *The Prophetic Intercessor*, is of such strategic importance. It deals with the power of prophetic intercession—praying God's will into the earth.

While some books, like my own *Possessing the Gates of the Enemy*, touch on this subject, none covers it as well as this one. James Goll is extraordinarily gifted to write on the subject of intercession and prophetic intercession with humor, integrity and deep insight. He plumbs deep wells of understanding from which others have given us only a light drink.

The Body of Christ needs this book. It is a next step in mentoring a prophetic group of intercessors who fight as warrior brides. You will want to read each chapter again and again, because each time you do, you will receive fresh insight and understanding.

I invite you to take a new journey into the realm of intercession with my friend James W. Goll. Open the pages of this book and drink deeply of its revelation. You will come away from it refreshed, encouraged, challenged and nearer to God than you have ever been.

Cindy Jacobs, cofounder
Generals International
Red Oak, Texas

Acknowledgments

I T SEEMS THAT I have labored over this book for years, since prophetic intercession is one of my primary life messages. I have carried this message within me for a protracted period of time, and now I feel like I have actually given birth! I was born for prophetic intercession! I trust that this portion of my life's journey will have an impact on you.

I want to take a moment to acknowledge two of the main intercessory tutors the Lord put in my life. Thanks to Dick Simmons of Men for Nations for his relentless cry for mercy, which I have observed firsthand. Thank you, Dick, for affecting my life beyond measure. I also wish to acknowledge my dear friend Mike Bickle, with whom I was blessed to serve in Kansas City for years. What an example you have been to me of keeping prayer central amid the swirl of many good things to do. Bless you, Dick and Mike!

I also want to acknowledge some of the others who have had an impact on my journey as an intercessor over the years: Mahesh Chavda, for his spirit of courage and sacrifice; Dutch Sheets, for his warrior anointing; Cindy Jacobs, for her precision in discernment; Beth Alves, for teaching us the "prayer shield"; Peter Wagner, for his skill with childlike faith; Lou Engle, for his relentless pursuit of God; Mickey Robinson, for his spirit of encouragement; and Pat Gastineau, for her wisdom from the trenches.

I also want to thank all the past and present staff and board of directors of Encounters Network. You have lifted up the arms of Michal Ann and me to aid us in our many endeavors. You have been such a source of strength and blessing in many times of need. I particularly want to mention David Sluka, my devotional writing assistant. What a treasure you are! I love working with all of you. Thank you!

Last, I wish to thank Jane Campbell, editorial director of Chosen Books, for seeing me as a diamond in the rough and being willing to tutor me in the creative ways of writing. You make this tedious process so much fun! You help me to b-r-e-a-t-h-e.

I am deeply indebted to each of you. Thank You, Lord, for the privilege of walking with others.

James W. Goll

PART 1

A Heart for Intercession

1

Marching on Our Knees

I T'S A BOY!" our doctor excitedly declared as our firstborn came forth. It was the Day of Atonement, October 4, 1983, at Johnson County Memorial Hospital in Warrensburg, Missouri. Intercessors had prayed around the clock at the hospital—on-site with insight, we call it today—for the successful birth to occur. Truly, a time of new beginnings had finally arrived for the Goll household as Justin Wayne weighed in at eight pounds, six ounces.

It seemed as though my wife and I had waited an eternity for this bundle of joy. You see, in the second year of our marriage, the Lord had given me a dream: *You will have a son and his name will be called Justin.* We would find out later that, according to the doctors, it was impossible for us to have children. Often, in our journey of healing from this devastating news, we had been bombarded with thoughts such as, *Is the prophetic promise still true?*

But finally, after seven years of barrenness, God miraculously opened Michal Ann's womb! Indeed, it took a supernatural event to bring God's promise into being. How about you? Has God given you promises only to allow your circumstances to get worse before they get better?

What does our personal testimony have to do with a book called *The Prophetic Intercessor*? Everything! This true-life story of our supernatural healing is a perfect illustration of the ways of God, joining the revelatory gifts of the Holy Spirit and the authoritative power of intercessory prayer. Our circumstances screamed in our faces, *No way!* But with God, there *is* a way. Circumstances might also be screaming in your face today—but *The Prophetic Intercessor* holds keys to change lives and affect nations.

So hold on to this sketch of our personal testimony, and I will fill in the blank spots in the next chapter, "Expecting a Promise." First let me share with you some of my beginning steps in becoming one of the pioneers of prophetic intercession in this generation.

Now hold on to your hat—because this has been one wild ride!

A Place of Beginning

Hey, we all start somewhere! I began my Christian walk by singing the songs of the church. Before I even started elementary school I was singing anthems from my brownish-red Cokesbury hymnal as loudly as I could.

I grew up in a Midwest rural community where they probably added the number of dogs and cats in the town to come up with the grand total population of 259. I was raised in church and it seemed like I lived my life there. It helped that Dad was treasurer of the board, Mom was the president of Women's Society of Christian Service, and both cleaned the building, mowed the lawns and did a whole lot of other tasks. Why, we spent so much time there that I was practically a church mouse, a regular fixture.

During my growing-up years in Missouri, I did all the things kids do in church—made paper airplanes out of the bulletins, tried to listen to those things called sermons, watched the older folks nod off and wondered how that head could stay on that stem of a neck when it bobbed so much! I also loved to sing the hymns of the Church. Today I have a T-shirt that says, *Real Men Sing Real Loud*. That's me. I think I must have sung before I walked! As I look back on that time in the Cowgill Methodist Church, I am grateful. Some good old-fashioned cement was poured into my foundation in those years.

I have since learned that many of the great anthems of the past contain rich church history and doctrinal understanding. But there is one hymn I would tweak a bit if I could. Now hold on to your hat. It is "Standing on the Promises":

> Standing, standing,
> Standing on the promises of God my Savior;
> Standing, standing,
> I'm standing on the promises of God.[1]

Hey, I know these words are biblical. After all, the apostle Peter wrote that God "has granted to us His precious and magnificent promises" (2 Peter 1:4). And Paul, the beloved apostle, penned, "Put on God's complete armor, that you may be able to resist and stand your ground on the evil day [of danger], and, having done all [the crisis demands], to stand [firmly in your place]. Stand therefore [hold your ground]" (Ephesians 6:13–14, AMPLIFIED). We are called to stand our ground and not give an inch to the devil.

Yes, I do love that great hymn and have sung it many times with all my heart. Also, like you, I have been taught that I must put on the full armor of God. But before you flip out, let me tell you how I would adjust that marvelous hymn "chiropractically":

> Kneeling, kneeling,
> Kneeling on the promises of God my Savior;
> Kneeling, kneeling,
> I'm kneeling on the promises of God.

Whew! I think you are still with me. In fact, I hope that by the time you finish reading this book, you will be humming right along.

Now let me fill you in on some secrets of kneeling.

You're Marching on Your What?

I think I just heard someone ask, "Why the title 'Marching on Our Knees' for this chapter? Aren't you taking this concept a bit far—kneeling versus standing? What's the big deal, anyway?" Let's consider this for a moment.

Kneeling signifies dependency. Kneeling is a posture of humility and brokenness. Kneeling is a sign of reverence and honor. Kneeling is the act of worship that precedes effective petitioning.

Prayer leader Dick Eastman stated in his first book, *No Easy Road*, that "those who learn to kneel in humility and weakness will soon feel God's supernatural power. The man of prayer is the man of power." Eastman went on to quote some beautiful lines by Richard Chenevix Trench that deliver a simple message:

> We kneel—and all about us seems to lower;
> We rise—and all, the distant and the near,
> Stands forth in sunny outline, brave and clear.
> We kneel, how weak! We rise, how full of power![2]

Kneeling is an outward expression of an inward work of grace. In fact, before Paul ever tells us in Ephesians 6:13–14 about the value of standing, he frames for us the privilege of kneeling: "For this reason [seeing the greatness of this plan by which you are built together in Christ], I bow my knees before the Father of our Lord Jesus Christ" (Ephesians 3:14, AMPLIFIED). Isn't that awesome?

Now, I am not trying to impose another ritualistic routine for you to obey. I am simply holding a magnifying glass to a heart issue. Some of us today are taught to stand and shoot at the devil before we are taught to kneel before our Father. If we reversed the order, maybe our aim would be better!

Sooner or later we are all going to kneel. Philippians 2:9–10 portrays this graphically:

> Therefore [because He stooped so low] God has highly exalted Him and has freely bestowed on Him the name that is above every name, that in (at) the name of Jesus every knee should (must) bow, in heaven and on earth and under the earth.
>
> Philippians 2:9–10, AMPLIFIED

If all of us are going to end up in the same posture anyway, we might just as well learn it sooner than later!

The Act of Worship

What is authentic worship? What does it look like? Worship is an act of giving ourselves to God wholeheartedly, with our entire being—spirit, soul and body. Twelve different Hebrew and Greek words in the Bible are translated *worship*. All four of the Hebrew words, and especially the primary word, *shachah*, mean "to depress, prostrate (in homage to royalty or God)—bow down, crouch, fall down (flat), humbly beseech, do (make) obeisance, do reverence, make to stoop, worship."[3] One Greek word for "worship" is *proskuneo*, which means: to kiss (as a dog licks his master's hand); to prostrate oneself in homage; to do reverence; to adore.[4]

The first mention of the word *worship* is found in Genesis 22, after the Lord asks Abraham to offer his son Isaac before Him on Mount Moriah. Abraham rises early the next morning, saddles his donkey and launches out in obedience to present his son before God. After three days of travel, Abraham's eyes rest on the site of sacrifice. "Abraham said to his young men, 'Stay here with the donkey, and I and the lad will go over there; and we will *worship* and return to you'" (verse 5, emphasis added).

We often connect worship with music and sometimes make them synonymous. But there is no mention of music here. The only instruments listed are wood, fire and a knife, and I don't think Abraham had in mind to whittle a flute and play a tune. All he offered was sacrifice, obedience and faith. This is worship in its highest form—a life prostrate before God. Worship is about bending the knee.

Scripture continually emphasizes expressions of worship and prayer (see 2 Chronicles 7:14; Ezekiel 22:30; John 4:23; 1 Timothy 2:1, 8). The Bible mentions both prayer and expressions of worship as integral elements in the early Church (see Acts 13:1–3; 16:25; Philippians 4:4–6; 1 Timothy 2:1–2, 8; 2 Timothy 1:3–4; Philemon 1:4–6). Let's briefly consider three New Testament accounts of how people approached the Master. We quickly find a trend: *Worship precedes petition.*

First, in Matthew 8:2–3, we are given the account of the leper whom Jesus cleansed:

> A leper came to Him and bowed down before Him, and said, "Lord, if You are willing, You can make me clean." Jesus stretched out His hand and touched him, saying, "I am willing; be cleansed." And immediately his leprosy was cleansed.

Before the man brought forth his petition in tremendous desperation, he bowed before the Lord. No wonder the healing virtue of God came forth so quickly!

In another awesome demonstration of the mercy of God, we find prostration once again coming before petitioning. I do not believe this was just cultural protocol. I am convinced that resurrection power proceeded in response to faith, humility and true worship:

> A synagogue official came and bowed down before Him, and said, "My daughter has just died; but come and lay Your hand on her, and

she will live." Jesus got up and began to follow him, and so did His disciples. . . .

When Jesus came into the official's house, and saw the flute-players and the crowd in noisy disorder, He said, "Leave; for the girl has not died, but is asleep." And they began laughing at Him. But when the crowd had been sent out, He entered and took her by the hand, and the girl got up.

Matthew 9:18–19, 23–25

The third example comes from the Syrophoenician woman with the daughter who was cruelly demon possessed. The woman came forth with persistence, shouting and crying out, "Have mercy on me, Lord, Son of David" (Matthew 15:22). I believe the Lord did not verbally answer her in order to test her and see how desperate she really was. But she continued in her urgency and would not take no for an answer:

She came and began to bow down before Him, saying, "Lord, help me!" . . . Then Jesus said to her, "O woman, your faith is great; it shall be done for you as you wish." And her daughter was healed at once.

verses 25, 28

Oh, for those results today! But did you notice? Take another look. The Amplified Bible renders verse 25: "She came and, kneeling, worshiped Him and kept praying, Lord, help me!" Yes, she got what she came for. But she, too, first came on bended knee.

Does Jesus deserve anything less?

Four Biblical Definitions of the Intercessory Task

Before we proceed any further, let's review what it means to be an intercessor. Many teachers of prayer credit S. D. Gordon with the following statement: "The greatest thing anyone can do for God and man is pray. You can do more than pray after you've prayed. But you cannot do more than pray until you've prayed." Isn't that awesome? Intercession is the right to shape and make history, and each of us gets to step up to the plate as part of our calling as priests before the Lord.

To lay the foundation properly, let's look at four major Scriptures: two from the book of Isaiah and two from Ezekiel. As we do, we will choose four overlapping yet distinct definitions of the task of priestly intercession.

1. Being God's Secretary

Want a good job? I have one for you. God always needs good secretaries. There is plenty of secretarial work waiting just for you. Here is our first biblical definition of intercession:

> On your walls, O Jerusalem, I have appointed watchmen; all day and all night they will never keep silent. You who remind the LORD, take no rest for yourselves; and give Him no rest until He establishes and makes Jerusalem a praise in the earth.
>
> Isaiah 62:6–7

An intercessor is one who reminds the Lord of promises and appointments not yet fulfilled

What is the job of a good secretary? A secretary is an assistant who keeps track of the appointments on the boss's calendar. This capable assistant lays out the calendar, reminds the boss of his or her appointments and prepares the needed material so the job can be completed properly.

The intercessor, like the secretary, does the same type of work. The person of prayer searches through the divine calendar, the Bible, and finds the promises and appointments that have not yet been completed. After locating these, he reminds his Boss, the Lord of Hosts, that it is time for Him to fulfill His Word.

2. Taking Up the Cause of Justice

For our second perspective on the fascinating job description of these priestly intercessors, let's return to Isaiah:

> Yes, truth is lacking; and he who turns aside from evil makes himself a prey. Now the LORD saw, and it was displeasing in His sight that there was no justice. And He saw that there was no man, and was astonished [appalled] that there was no one to intercede.
>
> Isaiah 59:15–16

The second definition of the great task of an intercessor highlights another key principle. *Justice* is the key word to understanding this verse. A brief, distinct definition based on this Scripture is as follows: *An intercessor is one who takes up the cause of justice before God on behalf of another.*

We stand in the gap before the Lord for those in great need or distress, lifting a cry to Him. You can change society by doing this. Take your place! Don't let a caring Father God be astonished and appalled because we are pathetic, weak or nearly comatose! Let the zealous new man called the Body of Christ arise and cry out to the Lord. Take your place, O royal priesthood. Get in His face!

3. Building Up the Wall

Now we get to be masons. I am not talking about joining Free-masonry or any other organization attempting to counterfeit the living Church of Jesus Christ. I am talking about laying bricks to build walls of protection around our families, churches and cities. Let's turn to Ezekiel to see this picture:

> "O Israel, your prophets have been like foxes among ruins. You have not gone up into the breaches ["breaks in the wall," NIV], nor did you build the wall ["hedge," KJV] around the house of Israel to stand in the battle on the day of the LORD."
>
> Ezekiel 13:4–5

From this Scripture, I catch another glimpse of the defining purpose of an intercessor. *An intercessor is one who makes up the hedge, who builds up the wall of protection in a time of battle.*

This is, after all, a day of battle. Satan is "like a roaring lion, seeking someone to devour" (1 Peter 5:8). Spirits of darkness want *you* for their next meal! So here Ezekiel releases an exhortation against the prophets of his day. They were not doing their jobs, which meant the enemy could do his. Prophetic intercessors are needed to build up the walls of protection against the enemy so that Israel (and the Church) can stand in that day of battle.

Part of our problem is that we have not had watchmen on the walls, surveying the schemes of the devil. Satan and his cohorts have had free rein in many of our cities to do as they please. No guards—no protection.

But praise the Lord, things are changing! Guards, like Nehemiah and Ezra of old, are taking a stand for righteousness and rebuilding the walls of protection around our cities. This is an act of intercession. Through it, we are confronting the powers of darkness and commanding them to vacate the premises they have entered deceitfully.

4. Standing in the Gap

Let's take another peek at Ezekiel:

> "I searched for a man among them who would build up the wall and stand in the gap before Me for the land, so that I would not destroy it; but I found no one. Thus I have poured out My indignation on them; I have consumed them with the fire of My wrath; their way I have brought [poured] upon their heads," declares the Lord God.
>
> Ezekiel 22:30–31

Watch closely for our last definition of these prophetic prayer warriors, or you will miss its impact. Look at this verse closely, which comes from the life of Ezekiel. It is not just another rendition of the previous example. The prayer warrior has another distinct task: to fend off God's wrath.

We are to take our position between God and His people and between God and the world. People of prayer are called to build up a wall, all right—but this time it is between us and Him.

We are given good news, though: God is waiting for someone to persuade Him not to pour out His indignation. Amazing, isn't it? Who knows? Perhaps our incense (see Exodus 30:34–36; Psalm 141:2; Revelation 5:8; 8:3–5) will cause the judgment to be averted or postponed. Our prayers can also be used to cut short, lessen or delay God's righteous judgments. We can use our intercessory capital to purchase seasons of mercy. From here we derive our fourth definition of the intercessory calling: *An intercessor is one who stands in the gap between God's righteous judgments and the people's need for mercy.*

We have been invited into a holy wrestling match with God Himself. The Almighty searches for a people who will hold His judgments at bay.

Worshipful Watchers

The Holy Spirit is looking for worshiping intercessors and interceding worshipers. These two "gracelets" must be merged together. We must learn both in order to be victorious.

I have been to the very brook at the spring of Harod where the Lord sifted through the 32,000 warriors Gideon had amassed and chose just three hundred to fight the Midianites (see Judges 7:2–8). The life of Gideon is one of my favorite portions of the Bible. I relate to him and his need to see himself as God saw him—a "valiant warrior" (Judges 6:12). Like Gideon, I have often felt my head turn and wondered whom the Lord was talking to when He called me (just as He has called you) one of His valiant warriors.

I have knelt at this clear, winding brook—not on both knees, only on one—and lapped up the water like a dog. Awesome!

What was the Lord searching for that day when He selected three hundred soldiers fit to fight against their strong enemy? He was looking for worshipful watchers. He instructed Gideon to accept only those who lapped the water "as a dog laps" (Judges 7:5). Ever watch a dog eat his food or lap his water? He keeps one eye on the food bowl and the other on whomever is approaching. Ninety-seven hundred of the men who remained dropped quickly to both knees and knelt to quench their thirst. All they could see were their own reflections in the water. But three hundred other soldiers knelt with one knee bent. With hands cupped to their mouths, they were watching to see what was about to appear on the scene—a prophetic picture of worshipful watchers.

Today the Lord is looking for the same. He seeks those on bended knee who are watching and praying, acknowledging that God is the strength of their lives. They are intercessory watchmen on guard against enemy attack.

The Velvet Warriors

In times of corporate praise and worship, my wife and I often sing what we call the "prophetic song of the Lord" (see Zephaniah 3:17; Hebrews 2:12). Many of these songs are actually prayers put to spontaneous tunes, petitioning the Lord of the harvest for revival and the outpouring of His promised Holy Spirit.

One afternoon, as Michal Ann and I stood before a conference, I was catapulted into a spiritual vision and began to put what I was receiving—a vision of the end-time army of God coming forth—into lyrics. These warriors were marching forward in unity. I saw the troops reach the top of a hill with resolve in their hearts. They were broken vessels in the Lord's hands. The Holy Spirit seemed to indicate that they were "the velvet warriors" or "the velvet army." As the spirit of prayer was upon them, they were taking territory in the Lord's great name.

Michal Ann joined me in singing and we took turns weaving a beautiful song describing how the members of this army were invading the enemy's camp. They were proceeding more slowly than they had hoped—but march they did! In the vision, you see, they were coming forward, marching on their knees.

Yes, we are kneeling on the promises of God our Savior; kneeling on the promises of God. We are velvet warriors, those who come forth in brokenness, on bended knee, in unity, resolved in our hearts to take territory for the King.

God's end-time army will have an outstanding characteristic. Its strength will not be in itself. All its strength will be in Him. Yes, we are the fighting bride, the worshiping army of God. His eyes are scouring the earth to mark those who weep over their Jerusalems, to find those who know how to worship Him in spirit and in truth.

Stop. Pause right now at the beginning of this adventure. Join with me in asking Him to be the delight of *your* life:

Let Your eyes rest here, Lord. Anoint me to be part of Your velvet army. I sign up for Your calling on my life. I volunteer to be an intercessor ministering unto Your holy name. I want to see Your purposes fulfilled, Your Kingdom come to my family, community and nation. Give me the Spirit of prayer and supplication and make me one of Your worshiping warriors. In Jesus' name, Amen.

An Overview of This Book

This is indeed a unique read. It is a book for our current days and those that lie ahead. It is about the merging of the priestly and prophetic ministries at the point of prayer.

In this first section, "A Heart for Intercession," we gaze at the importance of kneeling before our Father. This is not just some ceremonial task we perform and then say, "Been there, done that—even got the T-shirt." It is the prayer of the heart to which the Lord responds.

In the second chapter we see how the Lord Jesus, who "is the same yesterday and today and forever" (Hebrews 13:8), changed the medical pronouncement of barrenness and enabled Michal Ann to bring forth four fine arrows in our quiver. In chapter 3 we proceed to the question, What moves the hand of God? We close out this first section by studying the intense forms of prayer from the Scriptures and church history that are often termed *travail*.

The unusual material in the second section, "A Heart for the Prophetic," starts off with a clarion call, "Wanted: A Prophetic Generation." From there, I blow a bullhorn, "Calling all watchmen!" and further develop an understanding of standing guard. Next we investigate the subject of being God's secretaries or "Relentless Reminders." Finally, we glue all these concepts together with a historical overview of the founding of the nation of Israel.

Lastly, we turn the corner in our final section, "A Heart for Prophetic Intercession." Who are these prophetic intercessors? Not some new cult group! This is covered in the crucial chapter "The Lost Art of Prophetic Intercession." This is followed by powerful illustrations of "Crisis Intercession."

In chapter eleven, "Wisdom Issues," is material that could save your life from the perils and pitfalls that can plague frontline intercessors. In the final chapter, I close out our pilgrimage together by inviting you to "break open the way!"

A Prophetic Parable

This book is a prophetic parable depicting us—first as individuals in worship before our Father, and then collectively as the Bride of Christ—marching on our knees. The testimony of Michal Ann's and my healing from barrenness, which I recount in the next chapter, paints a prophetic picture of Jesus' desire to heal His Bride and bring her into fruitfulness.

It is often said, first comes the natural and then the spiritual (see 1 Corinthians 15:46). So it has been in my life. Natural healing preceded spiritual insight. May the Lord impart truth and inspiration into *your* life, as you ponder the treasure He has given us.

So, let the journey begin!

Practical Applications—Making It Real!

- In your quiet time before the Lord, incorporate worship before proceeding into prayers of petition.
- In your prayer group, ask the Lord to help you understand and fulfill the four foundational tasks of an intercessor:

  Reminding God of His Word;

  Taking up the cause of justice before God on behalf of another;

  Building up the walls to keep the enemy out;

  Fending off God's wrath.
- Encourage the spontaneous prophetic song of the Lord in your personal life, small group or church.
- Join with me in asking the Lord to anoint us to be His velvet warriors.

Recommended Reading

Love on Its Knees by Dick Eastman (Chosen, 1989)

Prayer: Finding the Heart's True Home by Richard J. Foster (HarperSanFrancisco, 1992)

The Worship Warrior: Ascending in Worship, Descending in War by Chuck Pierce and John Dickson (Gospel Light Publications, 2002)

Intercession: The Power and the Passion to Shape History by Jim W. Goll (Destiny Image, 2003)

2

Expecting a Promise

LIFE HAS SOME interesting twists and turns. Our proper response to those twists and turns keeps us moving forward.

Maybe you have a dream that came from God. You know for sure that you did not make it up, but its fulfillment keeps slipping through your fingers. Does this resonate with you? Take courage! We have to yield to the power of brokenness and then get right back up and fight. Remember, first we must kneel before our Father so we will have the strength to stand against the enemy.

This is part of what my wife and I have learned. As you read our saga in this gutsy chapter—a ride through history on the Goll Family Express—maybe some tidbits you pick up along the way will help you in your fight to see your own dream come to pass.

Who Turned On the Lights?

As I mentioned, I grew up in a Methodist home in rural, out-of-the-way Cowgill, Missouri. I was given a love for God and for the Church at an early age. My parents, Wayne and Amanda, were already proud of their two daughters, Sandra and Barbara, and wanted a son. Tragedy came when my mother miscarried a baby boy. But, as I have been told the story, she cried out to the Lord and said, "If You will give me another son, I will dedicate him to Christ's service." I was born one year later to the day—July 3, 1952.

I do not remember a day when Jesus was not my close Friend. Sometimes I say comically, "When I was born, I came out of my mother's womb, waved my hands and said, 'Hallelujah!'" I know that sounds kind of bizarre, but Jesus is all I have ever known.

Growing up against a country backdrop, I loved to go on long walks on the railroad tracks, singing with all my heart and talking with God, who was "up there" somewhere in the clouds. I just wanted to know Him and serve Him.

I was given three prayers in my youth that I often prayed—from the inspiration of Sunday school lessons, I guess. I would start out and ask the Lord to give me wisdom beyond my years, like Solomon. Then I would ask Him to raise up His Joseph counselors to the Pharaohs of our time, as He did in days gone by. My last prayer was that God would give me a heart of purity that I might walk with Him all my days. These great prayers could only have come from heaven above! I still pray them today.

In grade school and high school I gave myself to academics, singing and church. I may have been respected, but I did not always fit into the popular scene of the topsy-turvy '60s generation. After high school, while studying at Central Missouri State University (CMSU), I attended Explo '72 in Dallas, sponsored by Campus Crusade for Christ. On the last night, Billy Graham spoke at the Cotton Bowl on commitment. I, along with thousands of others, stood to my feet to declare I was volunteering for full-time Christian service. That night was one of the points of demarcation in my life. I was going for it—God and nothing else!

This is where I first ran into the Jesus People in a powerful way. Quite a culture shock for a country Methodist kid! But they had something that drew me to them. My inner being was intrigued. I wanted more of God. I wanted whatever it was they had.

The little black-and-white screen on which my Christian walk played out changed in a major way. (Today we call this kind of experience a paradigm shift.) Life was quickly colorized as I was filled with the Holy Spirit in the fall of 1972 and—lights, camera, action! Things changed and I changed. Today my kids would say, "Who turned on the lights?" God did! This skinny kid was now on fire and growing like a weed for Jesus. All I wanted to do was go to prayer meetings, read my Bible and get others immersed in the Spirit. I was now one of the Jesus People. I had finally found the place where I belonged, and I loved every minute of it.

Our little band of on-fire Christians was given use of a vacated fraternity house right in the middle of the campus. This sore spot was now turned into a hot spot, transformed by zealous believers into the "Jesus House." Everything seemed new. Life was an adventure!

The Plot Thickens

Young ladies? Well, of course, I still had my eyes open. But now my sights were set primarily on Him who died for me and had risen from the dead. Jesus was the passion of my life.

I graduated from CMSU in 1974 with a degree in social work. I went to work for the summer at the local hospital as a nurse's aid. This is where I met the charming Ann Willard.

She was a joyful, kind and pretty young woman who had just graduated from Warrensburg High School that spring. The nurses tried putting us together, but I would not think of such a thing. After all, she was only eighteen and I was now a college grad! But we took our breaks together, did Bible studies, prayed together and had great talks.

When summer came to an end, we went our separate ways. She started college, and I jumped into full-time campus ministry and another round of adventures with my best friend, the Holy Spirit.

That was September 1974. I did not see Ann (as I called her then) for nearly a year. But one Sunday morning the following May, I went on one of my favorite long walks, talking with the Lord. I remember the conversation extremely well.

I said out loud, to myself and to God, "Well, who's for me?"

I was surprised when I heard an answer back: *Ann Willard. Not only that, but you will be outwardly engaged by September and married on the following May 15.*

Even though I had not anticipated this kind of answer, the words settled down inside of me and I accepted them as true. And by the way, I liked what I heard!

Yes, the word that came that spring morning had been the voice of the Lord. We got engaged in September and were married the following May 15, 1976. Wow, how time has flown by!

A Promise in the Night

At the end of our first year of marriage, Ann graduated from CMSU with a degree in child development. I was already moving full steam ahead in Christian outreach ministry as a campus minister there. It was now time for us to consider starting our family. Little did we know the difficulties that lay ahead.

If ever I had met a woman destined to be a great mother, it was my wife. She simply wanted to love the Lord her God with all her heart, mind, soul and strength, someday be a godly mom and pass the heritage on.

Ann had been reared on a farm in rural Missouri, fifteen miles in all directions from the nearest town. She thrived in that setting even though her three older siblings were all boys! She was taught the fear of the Lord at an early age from her grandparents and parents, and a dear old saint she fondly called Mr. Tyler. Her family and its nearby country Methodist church—totaling eighteen people when they all showed up!—served her well. Her best friend was her Bible, and she loved spending hours with that dear companion.

But what a strange situation unfolded after we got married! The one thing she wanted the most, to be a mom, seemed to be out of our grasp.

We did everything we knew to do. Year after year we had the same results—nothing. We consulted doctors, took classes in natural family planning and received prayer from the spiritual Who's Who of the 1970s and '80s. We would get ministry but always leave the same way—with no apparent change.

Many trials and tests of endurance came our way those first few years. But we continued on our journey toward fulfilling our God-given desire, even though the sentence of barrenness was being pronounced over us. Desperation grew month after month in our hearts and souls.

One night in the spring of 1980, in our little home east of Warrensburg, Missouri, I had one of those short dreams—the kind you wake up out of and remember. It was simple. The Holy Spirit spoke clearly to me and said, *You will have a son and his name will be called Justin.*

When Ann awakened in the morning, I shared the dream with her. God said we were going to have a son, and He even gave me his name. What could be better than that? All right! We believed the good report.

I felt a total assurance that the dream was from God. A peace and gentle spirit of faith seemed to rest on Ann and me. In fact, through the revelation that came through this simple dream, we felt armed for the battle. Sure enough, we were going to have a son! After all, we carried promises of fruitfulness and healing from the written Word of God—promises like Deuteronomy 28:2, 4, 11; Psalm 103:3; Isaiah 53:4–5; and 1 Peter 2:24. We had praying people around the country standing with us. And now we had a revelatory spoken word—a three-strand cord (see Ecclesiastes 4:12). What a combination!

But circumstances did not change immediately, despite this clear little dream from heaven. In fact, circumstances continued screaming the opposite report right in our faces.

Before the Light Came Darkness

Have you ever noticed that in creation, before the light, there was darkness? How else would we know when it became day? Well, the path for Ann and me got darker. We were about to walk through what Christians of old have called the "dark night of the soul." Circumstances had not budged an inch. Though we still believed the message of the dream, we were beginning to tire from the roller-coaster ride of hope and despair.

A year had passed. It was now the summer of 1981. We had continued on our search to understand, through prayer and the medical profession, the path God intended for us. So we submitted to a long series of medical tests to determine the obstacles to achieving our goal. The farther we went, the more difficult and complicated things became. As Ann underwent a laparoscopy and other tests, our infertility specialist (tops in the Midwest at that time) found a condition he had never seen in any of his patients. There were multiple complications, all adding up to the reality that it was not possible for us to have children.

I can still see him coming out of the operating room, telling me he could not solve the problem through surgery or any other medical means. He could do no more. The long and the short of it? We had no more alternatives. In fact, the whole medical profession could do nothing more for us. The situation was dark indeed. We faced obstacles, numerous complications and no more options. We needed a creative miracle.

Well, at least now we had hard facts—detailed information. But we turned that detailed diagnosis into persistent prayer. Then we would pronounce the promises of healing from the Scriptures with a declaration of faith and command life over our bodies. We fought the good fight of faith, as Paul told Timothy to do (1 Timothy 1:18–19), by using the Word of God as a weapon of war.

As the months unfolded we were given many valuable lessons in "Prayer 101." Through the trials of it all, we continued to trust Him who held our hands. With gutsy determination, great brokenness and total dependence on God, we persisted in prayer, crying out to the Lord to intervene.

The battle raged. At times, all the "why" questions bombarded our minds. I had had it one night and went out on one of my famous walks. As I did, the Holy Spirit and Ann had their own interchange. As she described it later, she told the Lord, "I won't like it, but I yield to You my right to have children."

Immediately the God of all comfort answered, *I appreciate your attitude, but I am not requiring this of you. I say to you, you must fight for your children.*

Ann remembers it this way:

> As soon as I heard the Lord say those words, I was filled with the knowledge that the Lord was feeling my pain and that He longed for me to have children more than I did! I knew He was pulling for me! In a moment I became aware that I had been blaming God that I was childless. I realized very clearly that the blame really belonged to Satan. So I took a stand and made a proclamation that day. I said, "From this day forward, I'll no longer blame God for my barrenness. I take the blame off God my Father and put it squarely where it belongs—on the devil!" Suddenly it was as though a breakthrough had come, and I knew that significant damage to the works of darkness had been done. I was filled with new hope and with a courageous, fighting spirit.

So with new, holy boldness and armed with fresh faith, we continued in our battle to believe the impossible and fight for our dream to come true.

In the summer of 1982 it looked as though we had achieved our long-awaited goal. Signs seemed to indicate that Ann was expecting. But just as this happened, tragedy came hard and fast to Ann's family. Not only did her dear mother and best friend, Dorris, become severely sick, but Ann began to have problems of her own. She had to spend the next four weeks either in bed or on the couch. Our specialist, on his long summer vacation, was out of reach. On his return we rushed to the medical center, only to find out that we had possibly been pregnant. A sac was present, but that was all, so a dilation and curettage was in order. Sadness filled our hearts as once again we came home empty-handed.

These are Michal Ann's (the name she goes by today) own words about that period of time:

> We depleted every option we could think of in our search for an answer to our complex circumstances. Most of all we prayed. We asked God and asked God; then we turned and rebuked our barrenness and declared God's Word over our bodies. We did everything we knew to do—physically, medically and spiritually. Yet in spite of all of this, after six years, all attempts ended up in the same place—with no fruit.
>
> Let me tell you, it was incredibly painful. Jim and I were part of a small church in a university setting at the time. We spent those years praying and counseling with a lot of college students. They would fall in love, ask Jim to perform their wedding ceremonies and then, not long after, ask us to pray over their children as they dedicated them to the Lord. Meanwhile, our house remained empty.

In the fall of that year Dorris's battle with cancer heightened. She was a woman who deeply loved her Lord. One time she phoned Michal Ann, her only daughter, and asked her to visit. When Michal Ann arrived at the farmhouse, Dorris had a present for her, a complete surprise. Dorris had made a precious baby blanket for us! It was a beautiful yellow afghan designed after the original McCoy family pattern (Michal Ann's mother's maiden name). Although Dorris's days were numbered and her strength was fading, she had made the baby blanket in faith that we would have a miracle of our own.

What a sacrifice and what a gift!

A Touch from God

After serving as a campus minister for eight years at Central Missouri State University, I assumed the senior pastor role of our small congregation, Harvest Fellowship Church. One evening in November 1982 we were pleased to have a healing evangelist, Mahesh Chavda, visit and minister at our small church. I had met Mahesh some years before and we had become friends. He had also prayed twice for Michal Ann and me for healing from barrenness. He was especially sensitive to the moving of the Holy Spirit and was often used in the gifts of healing and working of miracles. Every year he went on two forty-day periods of prayer and fasting and, as a result, had seen Jesus do wonderful and unusual things.

As the special evening service came to an end, Mahesh began to release words of knowledge for healing. He gave expression to each impression that the Holy Spirit brought to his mind. The power of the Spirit was present and people's lives were being touched. As Mahesh was approaching the close of the service, he gave out two more words of knowledge pertaining to specific healing needs. Then he gave a final word—for barren women to come forward.

The next thing we knew we were standing on the platform, next in line to be prayed for. Our dear, gentle friend Mahesh moved closer to us. He seemed to be caught away, looking elsewhere for a moment. Then he said to Michal Ann, "Oh, I see you as a joyful mother of three children."

The power of the Holy Spirit came on us, and at the same moment, we fell like timber to the floor. The presence of the Lord Jesus was so strong and tangibly powerful that we were unable to stand to our feet. We had been trying to believe God for one child. Now Mahesh said he saw three! One thing we knew for sure. We had been touched by the living presence of our Master, Jesus.

Over the next few mornings, when Michal Ann awakened, she told me she felt warmth in her midsection. She actually felt pulling and stretching in her stomach region. It seemed as though she were coming out from under spiritual anesthesia.

As Thanksgiving approached, Dorris took a serious turn for the worse. For the next few weeks Michal Ann, joined by her brothers and other family members, was at the side of her ailing mom.

When we all gathered at her family's farmhouse for what was to be our last Christmas together, Dorris displayed what some would call intuition or maybe even a hallucination! Someone in the room, she remarked, was expecting.

Well, we looked around the room, and nothing fit! No one knew what to do with the comment.

Dorris graduated to heaven right after Christmas that year. She had been a godly wife, mother, friend, schoolteacher and ambassador of Christ. Michal Ann's heart was heavy. She had lost not only her mother but her best friend.

Right after the first of the year, just after we had buried her mom and were in a time of grief, Michal Ann caught the flu. Was she ever sick! I prayed for her and she got even sicker. I would say, "Come out! Leave her!" And boy, did it ever! Get the picture? This continued for days. I did not seem to be a man of any profound gifting. Instead of the Midas touch, it seemed I had the bad touch! The more I prayed, the sicker she got.

Finally one day I said to Michal Ann, "I'm taking you to the doctor. We're going to find out what this thing is."

This Is the Real Thing!

So off we went to the doctor. He knew our case inside out, plus the fact that Michal Ann's mom had just passed away from cancer and that Michal Ann was her only daughter. He did some typical tests, and then returned to the examination room.

"I have some news for you," said the pious-faced doctor. "This is the kind of sickness that's not going to leave for a long time." He paused soberly, and then took a deep breath. "This is the real thing."

What was he trying to say?

Then he added with a twinkle in his eye, "You're going to have a baby!"

We were both elated and shocked. I think our jaws dropped to the floor.

It was true. The following Day of Atonement, October 4, 1983, our firstborn son, Justin Wayne, came into the world.

I know the angels sang that day. I know *we* did! And in heaven Dorris was peering over the banister and saying, "I knew it! That's my grandson!"

Remember the baby afghan? Sure enough, as proud parents we wrapped our sweet little son in that baby blanket about one year to the date Dorris gave it to us. Holding him in that family treasure, we dedicated Justin to the Lord.

Interpreting Our Life's Journey

May I give you one more update in the Goll family saga? Even though the Lord had spoken to Michal Ann's heart that she must fight for her children, the touch we received from the Lord did not, for whatever reasons, fix all the plumbing permanently. We had to continue to kneel on the promises and then rise up in faith and fight for our inheritance. Each one of our promised three children, Justin, GraceAnn and Tyler, came as a result of prayer, fighting the enemy and supernatural acts of God's power.

But then number four came along! When Michal Ann became pregnant with Rachel, she went to Mahesh and said, "You said, 'I see you as a joyful mother of three children.'"

Mahesh just grinned.

"You must understand," he said. "In the prophetic you see in part and you prophesy in part. I was seeing only three-fourths of the part!"

It was yet another lesson. And today we are blessed beyond measure with four fine arrows in our quiver.

From the Curse to the Blessing

I might have confused you along the way, calling my wife "Ann" part of the time and then "Michal Ann." Let me explain. In these last few years the Holy Spirit has helped my wife and me understand that we have been walking out a prophetic parable for the Church.

Michal Ann was named after King David's first wife, Michal. Do you remember what happened to that daughter of Saul? She mocked David for dancing energetically in the streets as the Ark of the Covenant was being restored to its proper place and was struck with barrenness (see 2 Samuel 6:23). She was mentioned only one more time in the Scriptures.

A few words about barrenness: Deuteronomy 28:18 states, "Cursed shall be the offspring of your body," or it can be rendered, "Cursed shall be the fruit of your womb." Several other verses in that chapter, speaking of curses, mention that they may take the form of a lack of fruitfulness or productivity (see verses 23–24, 30, 38–41). In my understanding this surely includes barrenness—the inability to bring forth life or the tendency to lose life through multiple miscarriages—as a curse. One thing we know for sure: It is not a blessing.

But God will change the curse into a blessing. The name *Ann* means "grace." Our life story involves, in part, the power of God to change this curse into a blessing by His great grace. And guess what? The name *Michal* actually means "stream or brook." Today, instead of being barren, our lives have been changed to become a stream of grace for other people. So now my fighting bride graciously goes by her whole name—Michal Ann.

A Modern-Day Parable

The prophetic parable based on the testimony of our lives is also a message to the corporate Church. We could have stopped at any point along the way, thrown up our hands and said, "We quit! This just isn't fair!" But by His grace we continued to believe our dream, even when obstacles loomed right in our faces. My fighting bride, Michal Ann, modeled herself after the warrior brides who had gone before: "By faith even Sarah herself received ability to conceive . . . since she considered Him faithful who had promised" (Hebrews 11:11).

Today God wants to heal other barren women just as He healed my dear wife. This in itself becomes a prophetic picture for us of His great desire to heal, change and empower the greatest woman of the Bible—the Bride of Christ. He will arouse our love and plant the seed of His Word within our womb and bring forth the miraculous. He will put "the Spirit of grace and of supplication" in us (Zechariah 12:10) so that the dream called revival—a stream of grace—will flow across the globe.

The Spirit of Prayer

During the roller-coaster ride and the trials, something was imparted to Michal Ann and me. The spirit of prayer and the power of travail were put into our souls. I know for sure that God is faithful and that He answers prayer. I get the awesome opportunity to watch miracles in front of my eyes every day. No one can take that away from me! Our Father God is faithful and He answers prayer.

I want to see the velvet army of God arise. Remember, worship comes before petition. The task of intercession involves reminding God of His Word; taking up the cause of justice in a courtroom hearing; building up the walls to keep the enemy out; and standing in the gap with a cry for mercy, mercy, mercy!

It is never time to quit or yield an inch to the devil. God's Spirit works in and through us "both to will and to work for His good pleasure" (Philippians 2:13). It is not about us; it is all about Him in this path to cultivate a heart of prayer.

Come and let His presence sit on you, and receive the spirit of prayer. Continue with me on this journey. Turn the corner to the next chapter, and we will spot another signpost along the way: what it takes to move the hand of God.

Practical Applications—Making It Real!

- Continue to seek the Lord for supernatural healings even in your barrenness.
- Ask the Lord to activate dreams while you are sleeping so you can receive from Him.
- Invite the Holy Spirit's presence right where you are, and enjoy Him!
- Read Lamentations 3 and such Psalms as 13, 22, 35, 42, 43, 55, 60 and 69 to meditate on the dark night of the soul and God's promises to see you through such a journey.
- Go to a conference where power healings are taking place and expect God to touch you or move through you.

Recommended Reading

Only Love Can Make a Miracle by Mahesh Chavda (Servant, 1990)
Power Healing by John Wimber (HarperSanFrancisco, 1987)
Dream Language: The Prophetic Power of Dreams, Revelations, and the Spirit of Wisdom by James W. and Michal Ann Goll (Destiny Image, 2006)

3

Prayer Passion

A s WE PROCEED on our journey of cultivating a heart for
prayer, I have a pop quiz for you: What moves the hand
of God?

This important question has been asked throughout the ages, with
a great variety of responses. Ponder it for a while. I am sure there are
many right answers to the question; faith is a correct one, for sure!
Purity, compassion and integrity would be other good answers to
this simple yet profound question. But let me highlight one strategic
quality the Lord looks for: desire.

Webster's defines the noun form of *desire* as "a wish or craving;
sexual appetite; a request; anything desired." The often-quoted teaching of Jesus on the subject of faith states, "Therefore I say unto you,
What things soever ye *desire*, when ye pray, believe that ye receive
them, and ye shall have them" (Mark 11:24, KJV, emphasis added).

What do you desire? What is your passion? What do you want so
badly that you can hardly live without it? James 4:2 says, "You do not
have because you do not ask." This verse could easily be rendered,

"You ask for nothing because you desire nothing." What you want motivates you! Do you have a deep craving within you that results in passionate pursuit? Do you want more of God? Do you hunger to see Him move in the earth? Desire is the beginning of the desperate prayer of the heart.

Maybe we need to back up a bit and ask another simple yet profound question: What is prayer? Ultimately, prayer is nothing more than desire expressed to God. One proper definition of *intercession* is "the act of making a request to a superior." So we could say that prayer is the act of expressing a deep-seated yearning to a superior, God, for things to change. You have heard people say, "I'm so desperate I'll do anything!" Well, how about reaching the end of ourselves so that we intercede as if there is no other option left?

Prayer and intercession are the passionate cry for lives and nations to change.

What Is Prayer Passion?

I am convinced that the last days battle is a battle of passions. The world flaunts its lustful passions daily without shame. But the Church has often seemed anemic by comparison. It is time for the Bride of Christ to be filled with passion for her Bridegroom and offer extravagant displays of love. What better place to exhibit boundless zeal and holy passion than in the place of prayer? Prayer is the bridal chamber of intimacy with our Husband.

R. A. Torrey writes, "The prayer that prevails with God is the prayer into which we put our whole soul, stretching out toward God in intense and agonizing desire. . . . If we put so little heart into our prayers, we cannot expect God to put much heart into answering them."[1]

What are some basic ingredients in the recipe for true prayer passion? Let me give you some of my thoughts, which have been shaped by the writings of Dr. Wesley Duewel of OMS International:

1. Prayer passion incubates in a heart of love.
2. It grows out of holy desire.
3. It may be a special gift of God, empowering you for the precise moment He wants to use you in prayer.
4. It often springs forth when God has opened your eyes in a new way to a particular need.
5. It may escalate gradually from a deepening conviction of the urgency of those needs and God's willingness to meet them.
6. It grows as you continue to give yourself to intercession.
7. It will revitalize and strengthen your faith.

Finney advised, "If you find yourself drawn out in mighty prayer for certain individuals, exercised with great compassion, agonized with strong crying and tears, for a certain family or neighborhood or people, let such an influence be yielded to."[2]

Some concepts are best defined by what they are not. Let's look at the other side of prayer passion:

1. It isn't always loud, demonstrative praying. At times it may be quiet or even silent prayer.
2. It is not synonymous with physical exertion. The effectiveness of our spiritual wrestling in prayer cannot be judged by our physical activity or stance. Of course, at times the use of various postures is fitting, and can help give expression to the cry of our soul. (But whatever you do, don't try to work up spiritual intensity by your own human effort. That does not help you or God.)
3. It does not guarantee immediately answered prayer. Many prayers are heard and responded to instantly without protracted praying, and many prayer desires of the heart are answered as you simply "delight yourself in the LORD" (Psalm 37:4).
4. It does not earn you better status with the Father. Fervency in passionate intercession is an outworking of the Spirit's ministry of grace within you.

Prayer passion begins when we bask in the awesome love the Father has for us, His children—the supreme objects of His affection. When you are in love with someone, you will do anything to get near that person. One song puts it this way: "Ain't no mountain high enough . . . to keep me from gettin' to you." It might not be the current tune on the pop charts, but it is the song the Son of God sings over His Bride. A revelation of bridal love makes your communion more passionate than anything I know.

Consider the words of E. M. Bounds: "Prayers must be red hot. It is the fervent prayer that is effective. . . . It takes fire to make prayers go. Warmth of soul creates an atmosphere favorable to prayer. . . . By flame prayer ascends to heaven."[3] The vital ingredient here is the very same prayer passion—the characteristic necessary to fan desire into a full flame.

Expressions of the Heart beyond Words

Has your heart ever been bursting with love for the Lord Jesus, so much that words cannot express what is inside of you? Sometimes when I am overwhelmed by the loveliness of His great presence, words seem inadequate. When I am captivated by the qualities of this man Christ Jesus, my heart aches and yearns with the desire to know Him and to embrace His ways. This is when prayer passion is in full bloom.

But sometimes love speaks a language that seems strange to us. First and foremost, you see, it is a language of the heart.

The Language of Compassionate Weeping

I think I hear you pondering another question: *Do you mean to say there are prayers of passion that go beyond words?* Yes, sir! Let's consider the power of compassionate weeping.

Several Salvation Army officers in the last century asked their leader General Booth, "How can we save the lost?" Booth stated simply, "Try tears."[4] Today, church growth seminars are held across the nation. They discuss techniques and methodologies at great length for successful, growing churches. You can pass out cookie cutters, but a compassionate heart is forged only through weeping.

Jeremiah 9:1 records, "Oh, that my head were waters, and my eyes a fountain of tears, that I might weep day and night for the slain of the daughter of my people!" (NKJV). Jeremiah knew the power of the language of tears.

From the Trenches of Those Who Knew

I love to study church history and visit the places where heaven has touched earth. I have been privileged to participate in meetings in Wales where a great revival took place under the leadership of Evan Roberts. Evan Phillips was an eyewitness to the Welsh revival of 1904. He tells the following about those blessed days and the presence of the Lord that was with the young revival leader:

> Evan Roberts was like a particle of radium in our midst. Its fire was consuming and felt abroad as something which took away sleep, cleared the channels of tears, and sped the golden wheels of prayer throughout the area. . . . I have wept now until my heart is supple. In the midst of the greatest fearfulness I have found the greatest joy. Now the bed belongs to the river and Wales belongs to Christ.[5]

One of the most famous of the great English pulpiteers was Charles H. Spurgeon. Consider this thought from a man of the tearful trenches:

> Let us learn to think of tears as liquid prayers, and of weeping as a constant dropping of importunate intercession which will wear its way right surely into the very heart of mercy, despite the stony difficulties which obstruct the way. My God, I will "weep" when I cannot plead, for Thou hearest the voice of my weeping.[6]

Saint Bernard of Clairvaux said, "The tears of penitents are the wine of angels."[7]

King David petitioned, "Be merciful to me, O LORD, for I am in distress; my eyes grow weak with sorrow, my soul and my body with grief" (Psalm 31:9, NIV). Again: "I am weary with my crying; my throat is dry; my eyes fail while I wait for my God" (Psalm 69:3, NKJV).

Our beloved Paul, the apostle and writer of many epistles, wrote: "For three years I did not cease to warn everyone night and day with tears" (Acts 20:31, NKJV). And: "Out of much affliction and anguish of heart I wrote to you, with many tears" (2 Corinthians 2:4, NKJV).

The heart of God for the city of Jerusalem is revealed through the Messiah. Luke 19:41 states: "As [Jesus] approached Jerusalem and saw the city, he wept over it" (NIV).

George Fox experienced something similar: "I saw the harvest white, and the seed of God lying thick in the ground, as ever did wheat that was sown outwardly, and none to gather it; and for this I mourned with tears."[8]

May we dig again the tearful trenches of passionate prayer! Let's follow in the footsteps of the revivalists of old and call forth this seemingly forgotten prayer language of the heart. Let the power of compassionate weeping lay hold of *you*.

A Desperate Prayer That Called Forth Life

In the past I have often had the blessing of ministering in the Czech Republic and getting to know many leaders of the "living Church" there. Let me share with you a true-life story about the awesome power of an "eruption of compassion" in intercession that called forth life.

In my travels a few years back I met a fiery revivalist named Evald Rucky of Libreac. The following report comes from conversations I had with Evald and his best friend, Peter.

During the latter years of Communism, Evald Rucky was a pastor in the northern region of Czechoslovakia (now the Czech Republic) of a small Moravian congregation in the city of Libreac. The totalitarian rule over that nation had just lifted, and a fresh wind of the Holy Spirit was beginning to blow. Opportunities for ministry abounded, and Evald was one of the laborers the Lord was sending forth into the newly opened fields of harvest.

Evald had been running hard and fast, with great results. Then, on a mission trip to Sweden, he was hospitalized with a serious heart problem. He slipped into a coma and lay between life and death. There were few signs of encouragement for his wife, who had traveled from Libreac to be by his side. His congregation, as well as believers across Czechoslovakia, was praying for the now-fragile life of their beloved pastor.

Evald's best friend and associate pastor, Peter, also came to Sweden to pray for him. In Peter's words, "It seemed as though I was carrying with me the prayers of the saints. I was the point of the spear and they were the shaft."

As Peter visited his friend lying seemingly lifeless in a hospital bed, the Lord let Evald escape the physical world to experience heaven for a three-day period. God showed Evald some incredible promises concerning His purposes among the nations. While his awareness was otherworldly, his earthly concerns were put on hold. Evald was able to enjoy hanging out in heaven!

Peter, back in the hospital room, stood over Evald's body. He had come to pray but could not compose a prayer in any natural language. So he began to weep.

As his tears dropped onto his friend's body, Evald—in heaven that very moment—suddenly became aware that he was a husband, father and pastor and that his work was not yet complete. He realized he had a decision to make. The next thing he knew, his spirit was soaring through the heavens and joining his body in the hospital bed. Instantly this Czech pastor was healed. The doctors declared it a miracle and released him without even requiring payment for any of the medical expenses!

Rejoicing broke out as a result of this modern-day miracle. A new beginning had come and an authentic apostolic call was received. What called him forth? I believe it was the power of compassionate weeping—prayer with passion from the heart.

The Spirit Helps Our Weakness

With this background of the language of the heart, let's consider the familiar passage of Romans 8:26–27:

> In the same way the Spirit also helps our weakness; for we do not know how to pray as we should, but the Spirit Himself intercedes for us with groanings too deep for words; and He who searches the hearts knows what the mind of the Spirit is, because He intercedes for the saints according to the will of God.

The language of prayer, you see, is a language of the heart and the heart is not limited to the vocabulary of the mind. I have often paraphrased this passage in Romans 8 like this:

> Often we do not know what or how to pray effectively, as we should. But as we admit our limited abilities and yield to the direction of our Helper, the Holy Spirit, God will give Him the language of perfect prayer through us that is too deep for natural articulation.

This is my description of how the prayers of *sighing* and *groaning* work. And they do work!

The heart cry of the Holy Spirit is just too deep for human words. At times the depths of the Holy Spirit's prayers become groanings within our hearts that express a prayer desire so profound that it cannot be adequately expressed in man's natural language.

About now some of you are thinking, *Well, maybe I can handle this weeping stuff. But you're going over the edge with all this moaning and groaning!* Hold on. I understand. I used to think the same thing. But consider the words of the evangelical prayer leader Wesley Duewel from his powerful book *Mighty, Prevailing Prayer*:

> Our knowledge is limited, so we do not know what is best to pray for in each situation. The Spirit's very definite and infinitely deep desire must be expressed in groanings rather than in our words, since our words are inadequate. Spirit-born groaning is always in accord with God's will. The Spirit could desire nothing other. But God can translate these groanings into His fullest understanding and do "immeasurably more than all we ask or imagine, according to His power that is at work within us" (Ephesians 3:20).
>
> God the Father understands the Spirit's meaning as He groans within us (Romans 8:27). Our weakness (8:26) is that our human words cannot adequately and fully articulate the depth of divine longing, just as our personality cannot experience the fullness and depth of the Spirit's longing. We can express it truly, but not totally. We are finite; He is infinite.[9]

Dr. Edward Payson, the nineteenth-century pastor in Portland known as Praying Payson, was one who prevailed mightily in prayer. After his death, he was actually found to have heavily calloused knees. By the side of his bed, where he wrestled in prayer day after day, were two grooves that had been worn into the hard floorboards as he moved back and forth on his knees in prayer. Payson used to say that he pitied the Christian who could not experience the meaning of the words *groanings which cannot be uttered.*[10]

Yes, God chooses to involve us in His intercession. He has chosen to prevail through our intense travailing. Martin Luther wrote, "Nor is prayer ever heard more abundantly than in such agony and groanings of struggling faith."[11]

Each of us has walls of resistance toward God that we neither know about nor understand how to break down on our own. Groaning is used to bring deliverance by pushing back the pressures of darkness. Groaning pushes us through tight, distressing places into the larger places of the Spirit. Groaning comes from deep within us and can be a tool preparing us for the utter abandonment that God requires.

Groaning is not for those who understand what they want to pray. It is for those who desire to reach beyond what they know or understand, the ones who "do not know how to pray as [they] should" (Romans 8:26). Those who are self-satisfied will have difficulty groaning; those who are desperate will have great difficulty *not* groaning.

Not only does the Holy Spirit have a deep love language that He will express through us, but He will arise at times with the righteous indignation of God and wage war through His people. This is the intercessory and spiritual warfare posture. Obstacles stand in the way of God's purposes, but the Holy Spirit will step up to the plate and pronounce the will of God through His yielded vessels, using a language that goes beyond natural words.

The Prayer Passion of Jesus

The writer of Hebrews gives us a peek into the passionate prayer life of the Son of God. He penned that Jesus "offered up both prayers and supplications with loud crying and tears to the One able to save Him from death, and . . . was heard because of His piety" (Hebrews 5:7). Did you catch the intensity and desperation with which Jesus let His heart be known? Yeshua was not afraid to let His emotions show. "Big boys don't cry" was not true of the Son of Man!

In an amazing comment found in Hebrews 7:25, we are told of the ongoing ministry in which Jesus engages continuously: "He always lives to make intercession for [those who draw near to God]." Amazing! For three years Jesus did miracles among His people on earth, but for hundreds and even thousands of years, He lives to make intercession. Striking, isn't it? Profound! Startling! I wonder what God is trying to say to us? However you analyze it, Jesus lives for prayer.

May the Father put in us the same relentless, pulsing heartbeat of persistent intercession.

The Epitome of Desperation

I marvel at the writings of John concerning the emotional agonizing of Jesus when His friend Lazarus had "fallen asleep" (John 11:11). This chapter uniquely portrays the humanity of Jesus and His deep compassion.

Lazarus had a unique relationship with the Son of God: They were friends. Let's set up the scene of this awesome encounter.

Jesus was with His disciples—probably across the Jordan River—some distance from the city of Bethany, where Lazarus had fallen sick. Mary and Martha, Lazarus' two sisters, sent word for Jesus to hurry and come to his aid. But the Lord waited two more days before He began His journey. The disciples could not figure this one out! But Jesus had sought the Father and learned that this sickness would promote the honor and glory of God and that the Son of God would be glorified through it (see verse 4).

By the time the Messiah and His disciples showed up, Lazarus had been in the tomb four days. But Jesus had His own agenda when He came into town that day. He came to change the spiritual atmosphere.

Word of Lazarus' death had spread quickly from Bethany, which was only two miles from Jerusalem, and many Jews had gone out to Martha and Mary to console them over the death of their brother. Emotions were running high when Jesus finally arrived and was greeted by the grief-stricken Martha.

With anguish Martha cried out, "Lord, if You had been here, my brother would not have died" (verse 21). Then she raced back to the house and called her sister, Mary, who had remained there. Now, in response to Martha, she, too, went running to meet Jesus, and the Jews who were there consoling her followed. Everyone was in turmoil; the atmosphere was full of shock and disbelief.

Upon finding Jesus, Mary threw herself to the ground at His feet. Can you hear her say between deep sobs, "Lord, if You had been here, my brother would not have died" (verse 32)?

We know the final outcome. Jesus spoke with authority to the deceased, decaying body of His friend Lazarus, and life came forth out of death. The miracle offered undisputed evidence that Jesus is the resurrection and the life. Darkness was overcome and light prevailed.

What Was the Prayer the Father Heard?

But how did events go from chaos and uncertainty to the manifestation of the Kingdom of God? Was there a bridge between these two points?

Notice the phrase "Father, I thank You that You have heard Me" (verse 41) when Jesus prayed. The KJV translates this, "I thank thee that thou hast heard me." Whichever translation you use, it refers to a past-tense prayer—something that had already taken place. Was there some act of intercession that bridged the gap between the chaos of darkness and heavenly intervention?

For a long time I could find no recorded prayer that Jesus offered up. Then I began to ponder this passage further and look more deeply into the language used.

John 11:33 (AMPLIFIED) begins with, "When Jesus saw [Mary] sobbing, and the Jews who came with her [also] sobbing, He was *deeply moved in spirit and troubled*" (emphasis added). The New King James Version states that "He groaned in the spirit and was troubled." According to Vine's *Expository Dictionary*, the Greek word for "groaned," *embrimaomai*, signifies "to snort with anger, as of horses."[12] *The American Heritage Dictionary* defines *snort* as "a rough, noisy sound made by breathing forcefully through the nostrils." Wow! Jesus was overcome with compassion and responded by sighing, sobbing, groaning—audibly releasing the weapons of intercession.

As you look at this story more closely, you can find at least three waves of the Spirit's presence moving upon and through the Messiah. He identified with the pain and sorrow of the people. As He did so, a wave of compassion hit Him, and He stopped, sighed, groaned and expressed His desperation to the Father.

Others, standing nearby, wanted to take Jesus to see the tomb of His friend Lazarus. As they started to direct Him there, another wave of emotion struck Him and He wept openly. He stopped, and giant-sized tears wet His face and probably His garments.

Once again Jesus attempted to approach His beloved friend's place of burial. As He did, He became deeply troubled and stirred within. Like an animal snorting when it is angered, Jesus, the Son of Man, sighed repeatedly and groaned in the Spirit. Jesus was desperate. But in His time of desperation, He yielded to the Holy Spirit, and resorted to prayers going beyond what Aramaic or any earthly language could ever articulate.

Finally, as this compassionate eruption subsided, Jesus lifted His head with confidence and said, "Father, I thank You that You have heard Me" (John 11:41). What was the prayer the Father heard? I believe it was the passionate prayer of Jesus' heart.

The Invitation Is Extended

So what does all this mean? Simply that we have an invitation to enter into the intercessory ministry of Christ that extends beyond our limited knowledge. In no way does our experience compare with the depth of Christ's propitiatory, intercessory act of the cross. That has already been accomplished! Nonetheless, we are invited to enter the depths of the heart of Jesus, and release sighs and groans too deep for man's natural vocabulary. Whatever the distinctive purpose of these ancient forms of intercession, just yield. Let Him do it.

With the close of this chapter we are heading toward home plate: the last chapter of this first section, "A Heart for Intercession." Ponder for a while our final subject in this first section, "Travail: Birthing the Promise."

It looks to me as if we are becoming extremely dependent on God through the power of prayer! Just the place He wants us to be!

Practical Applications—Making It Real!

- Ask the Lord to give you a heart of desperation, hunger and brokenness. A desperate life ignites desperate prayers.
- Cultivate intimacy in your desperation. Intimacy with the Father is an essential ingredient in fervent prayers. Ask the Lord to tenderize your heart.
- Listen and wait for the Holy Spirit's burden in a group setting, then join Him as He groans through you for His purposes.
- Ask the Lord to enable you to feel His heart and shed His tears.

Recommended Reading

A Time to Weep by Stephen Hill (Creation House, 1996)
The Power of Brokenness by Don Nori (Destiny Image, 1992)
The Lost Art of Practicing His Presence by James W. Goll (Destiny Image, 2006)

4

Travail

Birthing the Promise

WHILE MICHAL ANN was giving birth to our third child, Tyler Hamilton, now a wonderful young man, I got a dramatic understanding of what real, live travail is all about.

Do you remember her conversation with the Lord in the fall of 1981? She had said, "I won't like it, but I yield to You my right to have children." The voice of God spoke back to her instantly within her being: *I appreciate your attitude, but I am not requiring this of you. I say to you, you must fight for your children.* The Lord was speaking about our natural children, of course. But these lessons also apply to spiritual children and giving birth to the promises of God.

The Lord's words on that strategic day have marked our lives ever since. We did fight for our natural children and continue to do so. But on July 7, 1988, as we were in the labor room, we learned another major lesson about what it means to fight for our children.

Now, I don't mean to offend anyone, but I may get a bit graphic to explain the situation. The birthing process had been proceeding fairly well, and my wife was one centimeter away from complete dilation. Michal Ann was in the short but painful part of labor called "transition."

We knew what to expect. After all, this was not our first experience with childbirth. Michal Ann's pain level rose dramatically, but I kept reassuring her, "The end is in sight!" Yet my sweet, cool, collected darling of an almost-perfect wife was losing her cookies. The pain was not just intense—it was almost unbearable. Instead of continuing to make progress in the final stage of dilation, the cervical opening became smaller. The contractions, instead of pushing the baby down the birth canal, began to clamp down and enclose him. My dear wife was caught in transition for more than an hour.

Let me tell you, my own efforts were no help. I had been trying to comfort her but I did it all wrong. She began to scream out, to my shock, "I can't do it! I can't take this any longer!"

We had no choice, of course. We could not decide this late in the game not to have our baby after all. We were fighting for this child's life. All we knew to do was cry out to the Lord with all our might.

Intense is the only word to describe the battle Michal Ann fought. It was called *travail*! Finally, when there seemed to be no more strength left in Michal Ann, something else took over. She dilated rapidly and the transition was over in an instant. Out came Tyler Hamilton so fast that the doctor had to run over to the table to catch him as he emerged.

Since the natural realm is often a mirror to the spiritual, what lessons can we learn through the anguishing cry of physical travail? If travail precedes natural birth, does it precede spiritual birth as well?

When They Cried to the Lord

"At God's counter there are no 'sale days,' for the price of revival is ever the same—travail!"[1] This statement came from a man who knew

God's ways in revival—Leonard Ravenhill, the English evangelist and author of *Why Revival Tarries.*

The legendary nineteenth-century evangelist Charles Finney said:

> Why does God require such prayer—such strong desires, such agonizing supplications? These strong desires mirror the strength of God's feelings. They are God's real feelings for unrepentant sinners. How strong God's desire must be for His Spirit to produce in Christians such travail—God has chosen the word to describe it—it is travail, torment of the soul.[2]

Matthew 11:12 says it this way: "The kingdom of heaven suffers violence, and the violent take it by force" (NKJV). Sounds rather intense, don't you agree? This kind of understanding, let alone experience, often seems overwhelmed by our fast-food approach to God in modern Christendom. But hold on. This, too, is subject to change.

God's Responses in History

Like a spiritual historian, I have searched out the overlooked subject of the cry of travail. So let me dust off several accounts from church history, revealing that the power of travail in prayer often precedes the fruit of evangelism: spiritual births.

I found the following entry in the diary of the pioneer evangelist David Brainerd in North America, dated July 21, 1744:

> In prayer, I was exceedingly enlarged and my soul was as much drawn out as ever I remember it to have been in my life or near. I was in such anguish and pleaded with so much earnestness and importunity that when I rose from my knees, I felt extremely weak and overcome—I could scarcely walk straight.
>
> My joints were as if it would dissolve . . . in my fervent supplications for the poor Indians. I knew they met together to worship demons and not God. This made me cry earnestly that God would now appear and help me. . . . My soul pleaded long.[3]

Brainerd was a pioneer, leading many Native Americans to the saving knowledge of our glorious Jesus Christ. Accounts show him kneeling in the snow, pleading with the Lord and the Indians for their salvation. (Yes, Lord, give us more of these wrestling intercessors in our day!)

As I continued my research on the subject of the cry of travail, I came across unusual accounts of the life of John Hyde (1865–1912), a missionary to northern India, who often went into the hills to visit friends and pray. Friends reported that it was evident that Praying Hyde, as he was known, was bowed down with intense travail of soul. He missed many meals as he holed up in his room, lying on the floor, overcome with agony, crying out to the Lord. Often as he walked and prayed, it seemed as if an inward fire were burning in his bones.

It was from this intense burden that Hyde began to petition the Lord to let him win a soul to Jesus every day that year. By year's end four hundred souls had been won to Christ through Hyde's witness. The following year John Hyde cried out before the Lord for two souls daily. Twelve months later, it was determined that some eight hundred people had responded to Christ through this prayer warrior's ministry. Even this was not enough for the man known as Praying Hyde! His desperation for souls deepened, and as a result he began to plead, "Give me four souls a day."

Hyde's strategy to win souls was not typical tent crusades or large rallies. He went for each soul individually in a unique manner. He continued in travailing prayer until he had assurance that he had first won the convert. Only then, it is said, would Hyde approach someone on the street of an Indian village. Conversation would begin under the Spirit's leadership and before long both Hyde and the sinner would kneel publicly in prayer. Immediately, Hyde would accompany this new convert to a body of water and lead him or her in water baptism.

This pattern repeated itself four times a day as Hyde's burden led him to reach out to lost men and women. Multitudes found Jesus as this humble man birthed them into the Kingdom—first through prevailing prayer.

Most serious students of classic revival have been inspired by the life of young Evan Roberts of Wales, who at age 26 spearheaded a move of the Holy Spirit that touched the entire nation. Gripped by God at the age of thirteen, he attended nightly prayer meetings for the next thirteen years, asking God for revival.

In October 1998 I was pleased to minister in Wales with my dear, modern-day-revivalist friends Wes and Stacey Campbell of British Columbia, Canada. Our tour took us from the north to the south of Wales, speaking in four different cities. We culminated our outreach at a packed house at Moriah Chapel—the very site of Roberts's historic outpouring—on October 31, the anniversary date of the original visitation in 1904.

The Spirit of God hovered as we echoed the same prayer Roberts taught the people in his day to pray: "Send the Spirit now, for Jesus Christ's sake." Then we cried out, "Send the Spirit now more powerfully, for Jesus Christ's sake." Some were bent double in anguish as God gripped their hearts for souls.

At the close of the meeting, a resident of South Wales came up and showed the Campbells and me newspaper articles he had found that very day in the attic of his house, describing the revival activity of 1904. One lead article was highlighted with a big, bold headline: "Roberts' Soul Travails." It depicted the awesome sight of the Holy Spirit visibly taking hold of young Evan's being—in public view—as he anguished desperately for souls to be saved.

God heard Roberts's travail. It is staggering to realize that more than one hundred thousand converts came into the Kingdom of God in the great Welsh revival!

Yes, Roberts travailed for souls. Should we not do the same?

Eight Barren Women

Since you know the Goll family's true-life story of healing from barrenness, you can begin to comprehend how Michal Ann and I got immersed in this stuff. We had desire. We had received a promise. And even though we had had the sentence of barrenness pronounced loudly over us, we laid hold of the God of the promise.

Before our miracle occurred, I did a study concerning barren women in the Bible that really encouraged us. Guess what I found? Eight barren women were specifically healed from barrenness! They had several things in common. They were desperate. They cried out to the Lord. And each brought forth either a prophet or a deliverer of the nation. Let me list these eight women for you:

1. Sarah, who brought forth Isaac (see Genesis 11:30; 16:1; 18:1–15; 21:1–8)
2. Rebekah, who brought forth Esau and Jacob (see Genesis 25:21–26)
3. Rachel, who brought forth Joseph and Benjamin (see Genesis 29:31; 30:1, 22–24; 35:16–18)
4. Manoah's wife, who brought forth Samson (see Judges 13:2–24)
5. Ruth, who brought forth Obed (see Ruth 4:13)
6. Hannah, who brought forth Samuel (see 1 Samuel 1:2–20)
7. Elizabeth, who brought forth John the Baptist (see Luke 1:7–13, 57)

I have listed only seven barren women, while I told you I found eight examples. Who is the eighth? Isaiah 66:8 portrays her vividly:

"Who has heard such a thing? Who has seen such things? Can a land be born in one day? Can a nation be brought forth all at once? As soon as Zion travailed, she also brought forth her sons."

Zion is the eighth barren woman. She will bring forth her precious fruit as soon as—when? As soon as she travails, she will bring forth sons. I have often heard it stated that if the Church would cry out like a barren woman longing for children, then we would have revival. I believe this!

What Is Travail?

By now I am sure you are asking, "What is travail?" Let me try to explain it.

As it is in the natural, so it is in the spiritual. Travail is a form of intense intercession given by the Holy Spirit whereby an individual or group is gripped by a gestating promise that grips God's heart. The individual or group labors with Him in prayer so that the new life can come forth.

The definition of *travail* from *Webster's New World Dictionary* is simple: "very hard work; the pains of childbirth; intense pain; agony." I have found this definition accurate in the spiritual realm as well. Travail takes place after you have carried something in your heart for a period of time. It comes on you suddenly. It is preceded by nurturing the promise; later the strategic time comes to push that promise forth through the prayer canal. Finally you realize that the promise has been born, and you are greatly relieved when the delivery is over!

I have learned these concepts by my personal journey, by looking to Scripture and from those people the Lord has graciously brought into my life. Like you, I receive jewels of truth from others and allow them to enrich my own place of prayer before God.

One of these dear consultants is the prayer leader of Word of Love Ministries in Roswell, Georgia, Pat Gastineau. Let me summarize her teaching on the subject of travail and labor.

The prayer of travail is God desiring to create an "opening" to bring forth a measure of life or growth. If the "opening" was already in place, there would not be the need for travail. Just as the "opening" of the natural womb is enlarged to bring forth the baby, so, travail creates an "opening or way," whereas before the opening or way was closed. With travail, there is always a way opened for life, newness, change or growth.

As stated in the Scriptures, travail comes suddenly and leaves suddenly. First Thessalonians 5:3 tells us, "For when they shall say, Peace and safety; then sudden destruction cometh upon them, as travail upon a woman with child" [KJV]. God declares, by the Spirit, that He wants a way opened for someone or something. Then, as we yield and comply, God can give the travail that births—for as surely as travail comes, so will the corresponding change.

Agonizing and Wrestling in Prayer

Different people, ministries and denominations in the Body of Christ use different terminology to describe similar experiences. Those who might not use the specific word *travail* have spoken of "agonizing and wrestling" in prayer. Where are these ways today? Where are these holy wrestlers for our generation?

Perhaps one reason that few wrestle in prayer is that few are prepared for its strenuous demands. This kind of prayer can be physically and spiritually exhausting. You recognize what is at stake: the eternal destiny of an unsaved person, perhaps; the success of an urgent endeavor; the life of a sick individual; the honor of the name of God; the welfare of the Kingdom of God.

Once again, Wesley Duewel:

> Wrestling in prayer enlists all the powers of your soul, marshals your deepest holy desire, and uses all the perseverance of your holy determination. You push through a host of difficulties. You push back the heavy, threatening clouds of darkness. You reach beyond the visible and natural to the very throne of God. With all your strength and tenacity, you lay hold of God's grace and power as it becomes a passion of your soul.[4]

Remember the story of Jacob wrestling with the angel until he received the blessing? Let's look at that passage again:

> Jacob was left alone, and a man wrestled with him until daybreak. When he saw that he had not prevailed against him, he touched the socket of his thigh; so the socket of Jacob's thigh was dislocated while he wrestled with him. Then he said, "Let me go, for the dawn is breaking." But he said, "I will not let you go unless you bless me."
>
> Genesis 32:24–26

As Jacob found out, tenacious, persevering prayer eventually pays off. May we truly grow in the strength of the Lord to wrestle, as Jacob did, and win.

Scriptural Accounts of Wrestling

We do not know for certain what Paul meant, but ponder the following passage from Colossians:

> Epaphras, who is one of your number, a bondslave of Jesus Christ, sends you his greetings, *always laboring earnestly for you in his prayers*, that you may stand perfect and fully assured in all the will of God. For I testify for him that *he has a deep concern for you* and for those who are in Laodicea and Hierapolis.
>
> Colossians 4:12–13, emphasis added

The New International Version says Epaphras was "always wrestling in prayer." Wow! I wonder what his "deep concern," which was expressed through laboring prayer, looked like. One thing we are assured of: It was intense!

When Paul wrote that our struggle, or wrestling match, is against the forces of darkness, he had in mind the Olympic Games in ancient Greece. Each wrestler sought to throw his opponent onto the ground and put his own foot on his opponent's neck. The Amplified Version renders a relevant passage like this:

Put on God's whole armor [the armor of a heavy-armed soldier which God supplies], that you may be able successfully to stand up against [all] the strategies and the deceits of the devil. For we are not wrestling with flesh and blood [contending only with physical opponents], but against the despotisms, against the powers, against [the master spirits who are] the world rulers of this present darkness, against the spirit forces of wickedness in the heavenly (supernatural) sphere.

Ephesians 6:11–12

Clearly, when we combine the lessons of Genesis 32, concerning Jacob, and the Pauline epistles cited above, we see a picture of wrestling with the enemy, as well as with our heavenly Father, in the supernatural realm of prayer. One common thread in both accounts: Don't give up! Continue in your wrestling match. It's not over till it's over, and it ain't over yet! Continue in persevering, prevailing intercession.

"Elijah, What Are You Doing?"

One of my favorite passages in Scripture has been that of Elijah's prayer encounter in 1 Kings 18. I have preached the revelation of this passage in churches, cities and countries around the globe, always with the same result. The gripping burden of the Lord comes on God's people and a new level of travail—at times dramatic—is released in and through them.

The following, therefore, is a synopsis of our life message based on the tenacious example of Elijah. It is the bread of our lives.

Elijah said to Ahab, "Go up, eat and drink; for there is the sound of the roar of a heavy shower." So Ahab went up to eat and drink. But Elijah went up to the top of Carmel; and he crouched down on the earth and put his face between his knees. He said to his servant, "Go up now, look toward the sea." So he went up and looked and said, "There is nothing." And he said, "Go back" seven times. It came about at the seventh time, that he said, "Behold, a cloud as small as a man's hand is coming up from the sea." And he said, "Go up, say to Ahab, 'Prepare your chariot and go down, so that the heavy shower does not stop you.'" In a little while the sky grew black with clouds and wind, and there was a heavy shower. And Ahab rode and went to Jezreel. Then the hand of the LORD was on Elijah, and he girded up his loins and outran Ahab to Jezreel.

1 Kings 18:41–46

Let me share that story with additions from my own sanctified imagination.

It had not rained for three and a half years (see verses 1–2). The land was dry and parched. Conditions in the natural realm were at a point of desperation; and the natural situation only mirrored the spiritual condition of the people. There was no cloud cover and everyone was baking in the scorching sun.

In the midst of desertlike conditions, the burden of the Lord was coming on one of God's choice servants. Faith was percolating within Elijah, and he "went to show himself to Ahab" (verse 2) just days before winning a great victory over the prophets of Baal. Fire had fallen from heaven and all the false prophets bowed low to the ground, declaring that the Lord was the one true God. Elijah was ecstatic!

On the heels of this dramatic intervention, the man of God heard something in his spirit that was physically inaudible—a sound in the distance unheard for more than three years. As he listened, it picked up volume. It was a thunderstorm of gargantuan proportions.

Elijah ran from the presence of the Lord into the court of evil King Ahab and proclaimed boldly, "There is the sound of the roar of a heavy shower" (verse 41). Ahab went about his regular routine of eating and drinking. He did not know what to make of this strange man who seemed to be hallucinating.

Meanwhile Elijah went to one of his favorite places of solitude. He headed off to Mount Carmel—the place where God had showed Himself strong just days before. Positioned on top of the mount,

Elijah knew that either God would show up again, or he would be stoned as a false prophet.

So what did he do? He took on the posture of humility and desperation. By the leading of the Holy Spirit, he squatted to the ground in awe of his majestic God. The burden of the Lord increased on Elijah for a day of new beginnings. As the hand of the Lord settled on him, pressure seemed to build inside this warrior: Something was happening.

The next thing we know, Elijah was overwhelmed with the transcendent majesty of God. He hid his face in his hands and pressed his head down between his knees. Then Elijah issued a word to his servant: "Go up now, look toward the sea" (verse 43).

The servant departed and searched the heavens over the Mediterranean Sea. He saw nothing. Climbing back to the top of Mount Carmel, I imagine that he gasped to see Elijah under the burden of God. Cautiously he told his master that things had not changed. The prophet exhorted him to go look again—in fact, to look seven times, if need be. Off went the servant, hoping to see something rising on the horizon. Each time he darted back to the top of the mountain to bring his news, only to see Elijah with his face still between his knees.

The servant must have wondered, *Master, what are you doing?* But each time he went forth again, looking for some sign of rain—to see only the scorching glare of the sun reflecting on the sea. Back and forth he continued, until the servant, with feelings of despair, reported to his master, "There is only the glaring sun."

By this time God's grip tightened on Elijah's heart. He appeared to be in the midst of wrestling or agonizing. What *was* he doing? A cry convulsed out of the prophet: "Go look yet another time."

On the seventh time—the number of completion—the servant rushed out, hoping to see a change. As he scanned the horizon again, something small caught his eye. He peered into the heavens. Sure enough, a cloud had emerged—but only the size of a man's hand.

With fire in his being he ran back to declare the good report to the man of God.

There was Elijah in full travail, a desperate labor of love. The young man reported, "I saw it. I saw it: A cloud the size of a man's hand!"

I imagine that perspiration drenched Elijah's brow and fire burned in his bones as the intercessory burden began to lift. Then, in a prophetic unction, he declared, "Go tell that Ahab he had better hurry or his chariot wheels are going to get stuck in the mud! For I have heard the sound of a heavy rain."

So it came about that the sky turned black with clouds and wind, and there was a downpour.

The Epitome of Travail

Is anyone listening?

This is a fair question to ask. The God of the universe is speaking, declaring that rain is coming to end the drought. Is anyone listening?

Before any event occurs, it must exist in the heart of God. Before the rain came to end the drought, Elijah heard the rain with his spiritual ears. Even today God speaks first. This creates a spark of faith within a man or woman. Remember, faith comes by "hearing . . . the word of Christ" (Romans 10:17).

But Elijah did not only go out and declare all he had heard. He prayed the promise into being.

There are many lessons to grasp here—but let's keep it simple. God speaks. Man hears. Faith is sparked. Man responds to the spark of faith and prays the promise into being. Tenacity and endurance are required when the desired result seems to be delayed. Even when the breakthrough begins, it takes eyes of discernment to recognize it. We are not to "[despise] the day of small things" (Zechariah 4:10), as a cloud the size of a man's hand grows and consumes the sky in a downpour of mercy, ending the drought.

Yes, as we see in the encounter with Elijah, travail precedes birth. Travail is the posture of desperation. Could this be the missing key to worldwide revival?

Before we turn to our middle section, "A Heart for the Prophetic," let's make sure our focus and vision are clear.

If travail was one of the major ingredients necessary for spiritual breakthrough, surely it is an important principle for you and me. May we add travail to our prayers of the heart so that others can enter the Kingdom. Let the pains of labor come upon the Bride of Christ, that new life may come forth.

Practical Applications—Making It Real!

- List what you are desperate for.
- Create an atmosphere with a group where you are open and vulnerable to the Lord, and ask the Holy Spirit to come and release the spirit of travail.
- Ask an older Christian about secrets for cultivating a heart for prayer.
- Listen to my two-CD teaching "The Spirit of Travail."

Recommended Reading

Mighty Prevailing Prayer by Wesley Duewel (Francis Asbury/Zondervan, 1990)

Modes of Prayer by Pat Gastineau (Word of Love, 1997)

Releasing Heaven on Earth: God's Principles for Restoring the Land by Alistair Petrie (Chosen, 2000)

PART 2

A Heart for the Prophetic

5

WANTED

A Prophetic Generation

CONGRATULATIONS! YOU HAVE now made it a third of the way on our journey together. In this second section, "A Heart for the Prophetic," I will offer another portion of my life, like freshly gathered manna, and pray that it will fill your heart with the spirit of revelation.

What Is New Testament Prophecy?

Anglican bishop David Pytches states, "The gift of prophecy is the special ability that God gives to members of the body of Christ to receive and communicate an immediate message of God to His gathered people, a group among them or any one of His people individually, through a divinely anointed utterance."[1]

In his book *The Holy Spirit Today*, Dick Iverson, former senior pastor of Bible Temple in Portland, remarks:

The gift of prophecy is speaking under the direct supernatural influence of the Holy Spirit. It is becoming God's mouthpiece, to verbalize His words as the Spirit directs. The Greek word *prophetia* means "speaking forth the mind and counsel of God." It is inseparable in its New Testament usage with the concept of direct inspiration of the Spirit. Prophecy is the very voice of Christ speaking in the church.[2]

Prophecy, we could say, is the expressed thought of God delivered in a manner that no person in his or her natural talent or knowledge could ever fully articulate. The substance and nature of prophecy is supernatural, coming from the heart of God into the heart and mind of a person by the gifts of the Holy Spirit.

This wonderful gracelet is primarily for the purpose of edifying, exhorting and comforting those whom it addresses (see 1 Corinthians 14:3). It can be expressed as either premeditated or spontaneous utterances by speaking, singing or even writing; through the language of dreams and visions; as a word of counsel; through music and other art forms; or by any other manner of delivery. It makes the voice of God accessible for our time.

But a message is authentically prophetic only if it comes from the heart of God, magnifies the Lord Jesus Christ and challenges the hearer to greater obedience to God's commands.

Stages of Prophetic Development

As with any gift, there are various levels of operation within the sphere of prophecy. There can be the *occasional gift* that empowers an individual for a specific situation. There is another stage of development, where there is a more consistent flow of *prophetic operation* as the believer matures. Some are blessed to enjoy a more consistent *prophetic ministry*, but this does not necessarily mean the individual has an Ephesians 4:11 *office of prophet*. Only God can bring someone to this level of consistent grace that blooms over time. Training is also required.

At some point, after consistent fruit and recognition from leaders, they will officially commission the individual into the prophetic calling. This may be a gradual training process, or a response to a sovereign act of God. In whatever manner the process unfolds, gifts are given but fruit is borne over time. Gifts may appear overnight, but character is necessary to steward them. Character comes only by way of the cross, and good, ripe fruit requires time exposed to the Son.

A Prophetic People

I am convinced that revelatory gifts of God are for the many, not just the few. The Lord is looking for an entire generation of passionate people (called the Church) who will walk in the spirit of wisdom and revelation in the knowledge of the Lord Jesus Christ.

What does it mean to be prophetic or part of a company of prophetic people? God wants each of us to stay so close to His heart that we can speak a relevant word to different areas of society.

There are three major areas where we exercise prophetic gifts. One is the area of church gatherings, home meetings and congregational celebrations. This is equipping the Church. The second sphere is the secular community that our lives touch and influence: the marketplace, the arts, government, athletics, business community or just at Starbucks. This is expanding the Kingdom. The third area is speaking prophetically back to God. This is prophetic intercession.

This, in part, is what it means to be a prophetic people: building a community in love, walking under the Lordship of Jesus Christ and releasing the revelatory presence of the Holy Spirit into every area of life. Remember, the prophetic gifts of God are for the many, not just the few.

The time has come. Rise up, prophetic army of God, and demonstrate through the acts of the Spirit that King Jesus is the same yesterday, today and forever.

The Prophetic Cry of Moses

The pressures on Moses were tremendous as he led his complaining people into the Promised Land. His cry to the Lord is found in Numbers 11:14: "I alone am not able to carry all this people, because it is too burdensome for me."

But God had a solution to Moses' dilemma:

> "Gather for Me seventy men from the elders of Israel, whom you know to be the elders of the people and their officers and bring them to the tent of meeting, and let them take their stand there with you. Then I will come down and speak with you there, and I will take of the Spirit who is upon you, and will put Him upon them; and they shall bear the burden of the people with you, so that you will not bear it all alone."
>
> Numbers 11:16–17

So Moses went out and told the people the words of the Lord. He gathered the seventy elders and stationed them around the tent. Then the Lord came down in the cloud, took of the Spirit who was on Moses and placed Him on the seventy elders.

> When the Spirit rested upon them, they prophesied. But they did not do it again.
>
> verse 25

What an amazing event, yet what an unfulfilling outcome! With a stroke of the Master's hand, the prophetic presence that rested on Moses was distributed among the seventy and they prophesied—"but they did not do it again."

Thank God this was not the final word on the matter!

For some reason two desperate, hungry men named Medad and Eldad were left in the camp (see verse 26). Apparently they did not show up at the right place the first time. Nonetheless the Spirit of God came upon them as He had upon the elders, and Eldad and

Medad released the prophetic presence of God in the camp of the Israelites, where the ordinary, rank-and-file people were busy with their everyday activities.

When I envision this scene, I see two wide-eyed warriors, so hungry for the Lord's anointing that their hearts' cry was "Give us all You've got! More, Lord!" God saw their hunger and jumped at the chance to smear His presence all over those two no-names.

There is no indication that Medad and Eldad ever quit walking in the supernatural gifts of the Spirit and prophetic revelation. I see them like the Energizer bunny: They just kept going and going. Perhaps they roamed wildly and freely through the camp, laying hands on people and expressing God's mighty word, stirring up holy chaos.

But apparently it was a little unusual. The Israelites had not seen the Holy Spirit operate this way before. Some were probably excited. In fact, they were ecstatic! They had been praying secretly for something like this to happen. Some were uncertain but were waiting patiently to observe the fruit.

Then there were the others. You know the ones who seldom have anything good to say and have the wet-blanket ministry? Well, one such person ran and told Moses, "Eldad and Medad are prophesying in the camp" (verse 27), as if it were something terrible. In reality it represented something tremendous. All the Israelites should have been rejoicing!

Even Joshua succumbed to the wet-blanket syndrome, adding, "Moses, my lord, restrain them" (verse 28). This is like people today who say, "Hey, where's the order? Don't you know all things are to be done decently and in order?" They are appealing to 1 Corinthians 14:40. But whose order is it supposed to be anyway—man's or God's? Jesus never told us we were to control Him and His acts. We are told that the fruit of the Spirit is to control the deeds of the flesh like lust, immorality and greed (see Galatians 5:19–25). Too often we recite 1 Corinthians 14:40 as though it says, "Let nothing be done so that things can be in decent order." But it actually says, "Let everything be done!"

I am not trying to promote anarchy, doing your own thing or distrusting leadership. But the dove of God needs to be set free from His ceremonial cage. I have heard it said that if the Holy Spirit had been removed from the early Church, 90 percent of what they did would have ceased and only 10 percent would have remained. But I believe if the Holy Spirit were taken from today's Church, 90 percent of what we do would remain and only 10 percent would cease. Get the picture?

Besides, isn't the reaction of "Hey, where's the order?" similar to churchmen who, through the ages, have wanted to control the activity of the Spirit? That was part of what the Reformation was all about. The separation between clergy and laity was to cease. We are each priests to the Lord (see Isaiah 61:6; 66:21; 1 Peter 2:5, 9; Revelation 1:6), and can minister to God daily in whatever vocation we find ourselves. Notice what Moses said to Joshua: "Are you jealous for my sake? Would that all the LORD's people were prophets, that the LORD would put His Spirit upon them!" (Numbers 11:29).

Moses' answer revealed God's heart. Let me reiterate that the prophetic spirit is for the many, not the few. The seventy leaders at the tent prophesied only once, but God yearns for a generation of people like Medad and Eldad to arise with a continuous abiding of His prophetic presence. We are each to be priests to the Lord. But it does not end there. Each of us is also to be God's prophetic mouthpiece.

A sign for all to read should be hanging on the reader board of every church facility: *Wanted: A Generation of Prophetic People. Sign Up Here!*

For Our Day and Time

Centuries after Moses, the prophet Joel picked up the trumpet of God and declared that in the last days God would pour out His Spirit on all flesh (see Joel 2:28). On the Day of Pentecost, Peter grabbed the baton from Joel and proclaimed, "'Your sons and your daughters shall prophesy, and your young men shall see visions, and your old men shall dream dreams'" (Acts 2:17).

The promise of God's presence being poured out, Peter exclaimed, was to the generation of his time and to all those who would believe throughout the ages (see verse 39). In fact, Scripture clearly indicates that as the biblical time period called the last days unfolds, more of God's prophetic anointing will be released.

This promise will be fulfilled, I believe, in our day and time. Let a prophetic generation of desperate warriors arise! Yes, dreams, visions and prophecy will flow among the rank-and-file members of the Body of Christ. We will see "wonders in the sky above and signs on the earth below" (Acts 2:19).

Can you see that the prophetic spirit is for the many, not the few? Let your hunger be stirred as you lift your desperate cry for "More, Lord!"

I am convinced that consecutive waves of God's Spirit will continue to wash over us until Christ's Church has been saturated with "a spirit of wisdom and of revelation in the knowledge of Him" (Ephesians 1:17). Our Father God will not let up until His people are filled with the revelation of the loveliness of His dear Son. Does this sound inviting? It is! And it is for *you*. Join the cries of thousands upon thousands of others across the globe today who are crying, "More, Lord!"

Cultivating God's Revelatory Presence

Recently I saw a sign on a church reader board that stated: *God's Presence with Us Is His Best Present to Us.* Is that ever right! We must learn to be a people of His presence. To this end, I have found the old adage true: "Some things are better caught than taught."

You can catch a precious revelatory anointing by being around people of the anointing. You become like those you hang around. So hang out with Jesus, His Word and, whenever you can, people of the anointing.

I think I just heard another one of those questions: "What *is* the anointing?" I use the following sentence to describe it: *The anointing is the grace of God that supernaturally enables an individual or group to do the works of Jesus by the manifest presence of the Holy Spirit operating in, on or through them.*

Noted author and statesman R. T. Kendall demystifies this for us:

> When the anointing is working, it is as natural and easy for our gift to function as eating or talking with friends. The gift is always there but doesn't always function easily. The anointing of that gift makes it function with ease. . . . The anointing, then, is the Holy Spirit. It is really just another word for the Holy Spirit.[3]

Love the anointing! Get around it, rub it and ask God for more of it. Ultimately this "it" is not an "it." It is the living presence of the Person of Jesus in the power of the Holy Spirit.

A prominent evangelist of our day has stated prophetically: "The great men and women of God that I am using in the earth today are not being used because they are something special. I am using them for one reason and one reason alone. It's because they've touched Me and I have touched them."[4] Remember, as you reach your hand upward, there is already a hand outstretched downward. God is ready to distribute His grace freely to whoever is hungry. So hunger for the anointing!

I think I hear a question coming: "So if this prophetic thing is about a vibrant relationship with Jesus, are there keys to entering in?"

I am glad you asked that. There are several.

Opening Our Spiritual Eyes

One of my favorite passages in the New Testament is Ephesians 1:15–19, which says,

I too, having heard of the faith in the Lord Jesus which exists among you and your love for all the saints, do not cease giving thanks for you, while making mention of you in my prayers; that the God of our Lord Jesus Christ, the Father of glory, may give to you a spirit of wisdom and of revelation in the knowledge of Him. I pray that the eyes of your heart may be enlightened, so that you will know what is the hope of His calling, what are the riches of the glory of His inheritance in the saints, and what is the surpassing greatness of His power toward us who believe.

There was a ten-year period of my life in which I prayed these verses devotionally every day. I still pray them regularly—at least weekly. I am not one who, by sovereign gifting, suddenly began to see visions and have spiritual dreams. These have unfolded gradually over a period of time, partially as a result of praying these verses.

Out of this history, then, let me share some thoughts and reasoning with you.

In this passage we find Paul, a father and apostle, writing a letter to the church at Ephesus. If he needed to pray this prayer for the model New Testament church of that day, how much more do we need to pray it in our day? Paul prayed for these followers in the faith "that the eyes of your heart may be enlightened" (Ephesians 1:18). Other translations render this "that the eyes of your understanding [or "the eyes of your faith"] may be flooded with light." Wonderful! Pray the Word—it has worked for me and it will work for you. Expect, like a child, to receive His presents.

Yes, we need to be like youngsters when it comes to believing what we see with the eyes of our faith. I have taught our kids over the years that we all have two sets of eyes: our physical set of eyes and those of the spirit. I have also told them that mothers have *three* sets of eyes, including an extra set located in the back of their heads! One evening our family was sitting at the supper table while I was explaining this concept. Tyler was only about four at the time and believed what Daddy was saying literally. He promptly got up from the table, walked around the other side to where Mom was sitting and parted her hair inquisitively, looking for her extra set of eyes.

"Oh, Tyler, you can't see them now," I said. "They only open up when they have to."

But we believers need the eyes of our hearts open at *all* times! Let's pray, then, in the name of the Lord that they are opened up. Call forth the spirit of revelation into your own life, as I have over these many years. Let's each of us be a child and simply believe that we have an extra set of eyes.

Listening, Watching, Waiting

In order to cultivate a spirit of revelation—the prophetic presence of God in our lives—there is another key for us to use.

The fast-paced, instant society of our day is diametrically opposed to the gentle, quiet spirits we need to be people of revelation. The Holy Spirit is searching eagerly for those on whose quiet hearts He can write the revelatory words of God.

Listen with me to Proverbs 8:32–36, as wisdom speaks:

"Now therefore, O sons, listen to me, for blessed are they who keep my ways. Heed instruction and be wise, and do not neglect it. Blessed is the man who listens to me, watching daily at my gates, waiting at my doorposts. For he who finds me finds life and obtains favor from the LORD. But he who sins against me injures himself; all those who hate me love death."

These words are filled with life! Look at the three key verbs used here: *listen, watch* and *wait.* To contemporary Christians these words speak of art forms almost lost since the early Church. But look at the promises granted to those who will engage in these seemingly passive activities. It appears God uses these actions to direct us into His life.

The resulting promises:

1. You will be supernaturally blessed.
2. You will find life.
3. You will obtain favor from the Lord.

Great promises! Amen?

But the writer of Proverbs also includes a warning: "He who sins against me injures himself." This sounds to me like a self-inflicted wound. To sin is to miss God. If this is the case, it behooves us all the more to learn these less traveled ways of contemplative Christianity: listening, watching and waiting.

These are not hard ways. But they require a simple application of a word tossed out in the midst of the Psalms: *selah.*

Yes, just pause for a while. (That is probably what that Hebrew word means.) We must learn to quiet our souls before God in order to commune with Him. Remember, prayer is not just talking our heads off to God and telling Him all the things we think He has not done! Prayer is not so much something we do as Someone we are with. This requires a rare activity—actually pushing the pause button.

True prayer involves *selah.* We must pause long enough to quiet ourselves and bend our ears in His direction in order to listen. You cannot hear what another is saying if you are talking all the time. It is impossible! So pause. Wait. Rest. *Slow down.* You will be amazed how this alone will revolutionize your life. And you will find that these ancient keys open those spiritual eyes so that the light of revelation can come in.

Expecting God to Move

Joshua had to learn the ways of listening, watching and waiting just as you and I do. He was the choice prophetic vessel of the Lord to lead the next generation into receiving the fulfillment of God's promises. He, too, had to learn the art of prophetic intercession.

It came about, whenever Moses went out to the tent, that all the people would arise and stand, each at the entrance of his tent, and gaze after

Moses until he entered the tent. Whenever Moses entered the tent, the pillar of cloud would descend and stand at the entrance of the tent; and the LORD would speak with Moses. When all the people saw the pillar of cloud standing at the entrance of the tent, all the people would arise and worship, each at the entrance of his tent. Thus the LORD used to speak to Moses face to face, just as a man speaks to his friend. When Moses returned to the camp, his servant Joshua, the son of Nun, a young man, would not depart from the tent.

Exodus 33:8–11

Young Joshua was getting the best training anyone could ever receive. He was a doorkeeper in the house of the Lord. When Moses was no longer visible, the rest of the people apparently vacated the scene and went back to their tents and normal activities. The masses went in for the big stuff—the bells and whistles, so to speak. They were content to worship from afar and rejected the passive game of waiting around. After all, wasn't that just wasting time?

But to Joshua another path had been revealed. He learned the lessons of listening, watching and waiting. How? Waiting, he would not leave the tent of meeting until Moses came out from having been in the presence of the Lord. Then, watching, Joshua was the first to see the glow on his master's face. Finally, listening, he was the first to hear the report of what had happened beyond the mystical veil. Joshua's view of waiting was different from the view of most of us. He waited in eager anticipation that the Lord was on the move: He was going to speak, to show His form.

So expectation is the final key that changes the waiting game into an opportunity for the spirit of revelation to be activated.

An Opportunity Awaits You!

How badly do you want to see a prophetic Church arise? How much do you want the Church to take her rightful position in broader

WANTED: A PROPHETIC GENERATION

society? Are you willing to do the little things necessary to capture God's presence and be a person of revelation?

A test awaits us all—and an unprecedented opportunity. The world is looking for answers. But will we get off the fast production line of frantic living long enough to receive something that can be heard? God's voice rings with another sound. It is the sound of consecration. The sound of revolution. The sound of revelation.

What would it be like for people to have Holy Spirit–inspired prayers waiting to be echoed back into the throne room of God? How much change would happen if the Spirit of revelation were wedded with holy, persistent, believing petitions and shot like arrows heavenward?

The Holy Spirit is searching for new recruits in the army of God. The Lord has put out a big sign for us each to read: *Wanted: A Generation of Prophetic People.* Yes, such people are desired by God—searched for and desperately needed. A great hunting expedition is underway. The Hound of Heaven is on the loose, sniffing out His prey. We are His targets and He is seeking us with overpowering love and sending out His clarion call.

Why should we cultivate a spirit of revelation? It is not only important; it is necessary if we are to intercede effectively. How else will we know which of the chocolates from the Russell Stover box we are to pick? Do we select just any of the promises from God's Word to hang on our refrigerators or mirrors and pray back to Him?

First, though, will you sign up right now to be a Medad or Eldad for your generation? Will you dare to take God's revelatory presence into the marketplace and affect the world as no generation ever has before?

The velvet warriors are arising and moving forward on their knees. I think I can hear them travailing as they cry for God's prophetic presence to be flung on them as it was on the elders of Moses' day: "More, Lord! Don't forget me!"

Practical Applications—Making It Real!

- Seek after the prophetic gift as directed by 1 Corinthians 14:1.
- Research the Scriptures on visions. Ask the Lord to release them to you.
- Go to a prophetic conference to receive further impartation from the Holy Spirit.
- Meditate on Ephesians 1:15–19, praying this back to the Father every day for the next 21 days.
- Cultivate a spirit of revelation by inviting the presence of the Holy Spirit. Then listen, watch and wait to see what the Lord will do.

Recommended Reading

Developing Your Prophetic Gifting by Graham Cooke (Chosen, 2003)

The Voice of God: How God Speaks Personally and Corporately to His Children Today by Cindy Jacobs (Regal Books, 2004)

The Coming Prophetic Revolution: A Call for Passionate, Consecrated Warriors by Jim W. Goll (Chosen, 2001)

The Anointing: Yesterday, Today and Tomorrow by R. T. Kendall (Charisma House, 2003)

6

Watchmen on Guard

SOME TIME AGO, I found myself leading a small prayer retreat in a beautiful, hidden-away spot in the state of Kansas. Our schedule was simple. We had no planned times of teaching, just times of waiting on God. All those precious hours were set apart for worship, intercession and reflection. I was determined that every hour we would have two or three people "keeping the watch." The Lord blessed our simple attempts wonderfully by releasing the sweetness of His presence as we gathered in His name.

Since the Lord has often awakened me at two in the morning to watch with Him for an hour or so, I kept watch during the 2:00–3:00 A.M. hour during the retreat.

During my brief watch, the Holy Spirit gave me a short but clear vision of a plow sitting among other old farm implements.

I asked the Lord, "What is this?"

The internal voice of the Holy Spirit replied, *These are the ancient tools.*

My next question, obviously, was, "What are the ancient tools?"

Another phrase came to me immediately: *The watch of the Lord. I will restore the ancient tools of the "watch of the Lord." It has been used and will be used again to change the expression of Christianity across the face of the earth.*

These words resonated within my being and left a deposit of faith within me. I knew God would restore the ancient "watch of the Lord" to the Church in our day. *It has been used and will be used again.* These words have continued to echo within me.

Yes, the watch of the Lord has basically been a forgotten model of prayer. It is a lost tool that needs the rust of inactivity scoured off and its edge sharpened. We need this great tool (as well as every tool we can get!) in every congregation and city.

My search led me to explore a tremendous treasure chest of knowledge in Scripture and church history. Eventually it led me to the Moravian Christians of the 1700s who founded a village in Saxony (today, an eastern portion of Germany) called Herrnhut, which means "the Lord's watch." My wife and I led a prayer expedition to the community of Herrnhut, where we had a dramatic encounter calling forth the spirit of prayer that rested on those dedicated Christians many years before.

Those evangelical Czech brothers and sisters were dedicated to "win for the Lamb the rewards of His suffering," and wedded the ministries of missions and prayer. Those persecuted believers stewarded an around-the-clock prayer watch that lasted more than one hundred years. While visiting a museum in Herrnhut, I read the following in a letter from John Wesley to Nicolaus Ludwig, Count of Zinzendorf. He was the young nobleman who provided land for these persecuted Protestant refugees: "When will this Christianity cover the earth as the waters cover the seas?"

Few English-speaking people today use the term *the watch of the Lord.* It is as though there is a moratorium on the subject. Yet the importance of the watch of the Lord, even the spiritual discipline of watching in prayer, is very important to the plans and order of God. In several gospel accounts Jesus commanded us to "watch" with Him (see Matthew 24:42; Mark 13:33–37; Luke 21:36; all KJV), particularly in the time called the last days.

But what does the word *watch* mean?

Be Vigilant! Be Awake!

In New Testament Greek the word for "watch" is *gregoreo.* It means "to be awake or vigilant." This is where we get the term *prayer vigil. Webster's* defines this meaning of *watch* as "keeping awake in order to guard; to give a close observation; to be on the alert; or to be alert."

Matthew 26:41 gives Jesus' admonition to His slumbering disciples in the Garden of Gethsemane: "Keep watching and praying that you may not enter into temptation; the spirit is willing, but the flesh is weak." (Similar words are recorded in Mark 14:38.) Paul's counsel is: "Continue in prayer, and watch in the same with thanksgiving" (Colossians 4:2, KJV). Luke 21:36 admonishes us, "Watch ye therefore, and pray always, that ye may be accounted worthy to escape" (KJV). The New American Standard Bible renders this verse: "Keep on the alert at all times, praying that you may have strength to escape all these things that are about to take place."

Perhaps the Holy Spirit is trying to get a point across! Watching is related to having the strength to overcome.

Two Main Uses

Upon further study, we find that the Bible uses *watch* in two primary ways. One describes a spiritual attitude of alertness in one's heart. The other refers to a specific form of praying. As one heart is revived and the fire spreads to others, we have the beginnings of a spiritual awakening in which the Church in a given generation awakens and arises to affect every sphere of society.

We must embrace both meanings and become vigilant in our prayer watching. We must join our works with our faith, go into the world and wake it up with the powerful truth of the Gospel.

Prophetic watchmen can be compared to the night watchmen or security guards of our day. They patrol our cities and guard important places of business while others sleep. They stay awake so that thieves or intruders cannot gain entrance. If a thief does attempt to break in, he will be caught if someone is alert. You see, watchmen are awake on behalf of another.

Watching is to sleeping as fasting is to eating—a sacrifice we make on behalf of another. Watching can also be a weapon of the Holy Spirit in spiritual warfare, and a form of intercession. Watching in the spirit is a powerful tool to bring us into deeper personal communion with our Lord. I love listening, watching and waiting for my Beloved.

Continuous Movement

There is another reason we must be awake or vigilant. There is continuous movement in the kingdom of darkness and in the Kingdom of light. The very first mention of the Holy Spirit in the Bible reveals this as part of His nature: "The Spirit of God was moving over the surface of the waters" (Genesis 1:2). God the Holy Spirit has been moving from the beginning and has never stopped.

The devil and his demons are also in constant motion. Jesus told us that once a spirit has been cast out of its abode, it seeks rest but cannot find it. If the defeated demonic forces do not locate another habitation, they try to come back with more of their buddies (see Matthew 12:43–45).

We find an Old Testament development of this understanding in the book of Daniel. The prophet was told by his heavenly emissary: "I shall now return to fight against the prince of Persia; so I am going forth, and behold, the prince of Greece is about to come" (Daniel 10:20). The prince of Persia, a demonic power, had already opposed this angelic messenger (see verse 13), and now the prince of Greece was about to enter the scene as a major world power. As the book of Daniel parts the curtains of history for us, we see a larger view of this movement among the supernatural forces. Spirits, you see, are constantly on the move.

Neither God and His army nor Satan and his league are stagnant. We must open up our spiritual eyes in order to watch their activities. While the enemy always comes "to steal and kill and destroy" (John 10:10), he does not always use the same tactic. Paul said, "We are not ignorant of [Satan's] schemes" (2 Corinthians 2:11). Let's keep awake, then, in order to guard. Peter understood this concept and warned us of the enemies prowling about in the spirit realm:

> Be self-controlled and alert. Your enemy the devil prowls around like a roaring lion looking for someone to devour. Resist him, standing firm in the faith, because you know that your brothers throughout the world are undergoing the same kind of sufferings.
>
> 1 Peter 5:8–9, NIV

Here we are exhorted, in the words of the New American Standard Bible, to have a "sober spirit," to "be on the alert," to "resist" the devil and to stand firm. The devil does not stand still. Don't be caught off guard by expecting the same stuff from the same ol' enemy. He is smarter than that!

Specific Watches Listed in Scripture

Historically and biblically, *the watch* is a military term used to define segments of time during which sentries guarded their cities from harm, alerted the citizens of approaching enemies or even welcomed ambassadors of goodwill. These guards remained in their places until their watches were complete and other watchmen took their places.

In the Hebrew culture, a new day began at sunset. The watch was divided into three-hour sections, with the first watch from 6:00 to 9:00

P.M. Since the Church has Jewish-Hebrew roots, this understanding was carried over into New Testament times.

We observe the Hebrew concept of the watch in Mark 6:48: "At about the fourth watch of the night [Jesus] came to them, walking on the sea." This early morning watch then was between 3:00 and 6:00 A.M.

Sentries are called to report what they see. They take their stations, guard the city and watch to see who or what is coming near. For example, a declaration of approaching horsemen is given.

Likewise, we need spiritual guards on the walls of our cities and regions. These watchmen will protect the community of believers from oncoming attacks of the enemy. Oh, how we need this ministry restored in our day!

Breaking the Powers of Darkness

Scripture gives us numerous examples of those who maintained some kind of hourly prayer vigil. These various watches also fulfilled distinct purposes.

Exodus 14:24 describes this scene: "At the morning watch, the LORD looked down on the army of the Egyptians through the pillar of fire and cloud and brought the army of the Egyptians into confusion." Many intercessors comment that the early morning watch, right before the sun rises, is a time of contention. In the realm of spiritual warfare, this is often the time that witchcraft practitioners release their curses.

On God's side of things, the early morning watch is a time to break the power of darkness and call forth the light of Jesus to overpower it. Early morning is a time to enthrone the one true God and declare His wonders through the power of praise. Psalm 101:8 spells this out plainly: "Every morning I will destroy all the wicked of the land, so as to cut off from the city of the LORD all those who do iniquity." Let the morning watchmen take their places!

Waiting for the Light

Psalm 130:5–6 reflects further on these various watches: "I wait for the LORD, my soul does wait, and in His word do I hope. My soul waits for the LORD more than the watchmen for the morning; indeed, more than the watchmen for the morning." My heart aches within me when I read this verse. A cry arises within me saying, *Yes, I will wait for the Lord.*

Here we are called to a higher task than simply looking into the enemy's camp. We are given a divine motivation that goes far beyond just watching the passage of hours. Grasp the higher perspective; we get to look into God's camp and see what He intends to do. Isn't it awesome? We get to wait for the appearing of the Lord and call forth His manifest presence. Oh, the glory of His brilliant presence!

The Corporate Hour of Prayer

Acts 3:1 tells us there were set hours of corporate prayer in the early Church: "Peter and John were going up to the temple at the ninth hour, the hour of prayer." When 3:00 P.M. rolled around, Peter and John knew they could get in on a prayer meeting, so they joined the other believers in this corporate hour of prayer. It was common knowledge and the practice of the first-century Church.

Imagine how tremendous it would be if you went to visit another city and knew that at a certain hour there would be a public time of intercession. No matter what part of the country you were visiting, you could locate the believers in that city and know you could get in on a prayer meeting.

May this, too, be restored in our churches and cities.

Three Times a Day

Late in the summer or early in the fall, you can hear some serious grunting and groaning all across the United States. What is this strange sound? I hear it coming from young people—teenage guys,

97

in fact, at football practice mornings, afternoons and sometimes even evenings. "No pain, no gain," they say. "The team that sweats together stays together"—something like that.

Others have released sounds of agony more than once a day, too—God's velvet army throughout the generations. King David offers an example for us in Psalm 55:16–17, an inspiration for many modern-day churches and ministries: "As for me, I shall call upon God, and the LORD will save me. Evening and morning and at noon, I will complain and murmur, and He will hear my voice."

The prophet Daniel was one who helped pioneer this model when he, too, lifted his voice three times daily:

> [Daniel] entered his house (now in his roof chamber he had windows open toward Jerusalem); and *he continued kneeling on his knees three times a day, praying and giving thanks before his God*, as he had been doing previously.
>
> Daniel 6:10 (emphasis added)

Morning, noon and evening, the sacrifices of prayer and praise and the sounds of deliverance are to ascend to the Lord. What a blessing! May our Captain hear the sounds of many more "practices" as the velvet army grows in strength and number from shore to shore. Remember, the team that sweats together. . .

The Three Stations

By this time, it should be obvious that God wants to clue us in to His plans and tip us off concerning the enemy's schemes. But we have a different vantage point according to what position we hold on the wall.

I have walked on the physical wall surrounding the Old City of Jerusalem. Each section stands at a different height with a specific lookout point and overlooks a different sector of the city. In this complex maze of religious and architectural wonders, you can see entirely different views of Jerusalem. It all depends on your position on the wall.

It is the same for us, getting our read in the Holy Spirit. There are many different angles from which we gain our view. Or, to change the metaphor, each of us brings a piece of the jigsaw puzzle, and when the pieces are brought together, we can see the whole picture. Rick Joyner expresses this wonderfully in his book *The Prophetic Ministry*:

> The biblical positions of the watchmen were (1) on the walls of the city (Isaiah 62:6–7), (2) walking about in the city (Song of Solomon 3:3), and (3) on the hills or in the countryside (Jeremiah 31:6). Together these can give us a good picture of the operation of this ministry.
>
> The Lord has called spiritual watchmen today who are to serve in each of these three positions. He has some whose only purpose is to be watching within the church for the movement of the King, and to make a way for Him. These are also called to recognize and report to the elders any disorderly or unlawful behavior. There are also some who have been given a place of vision that enables them to see both inside and outside of the church. And some watchmen are called mainly to roam around as scouts in the world, able to spot such things as the rise of a new cult or a major persecution against the church.[1]

Praying On-Site with Insight

Among the old implements that have been used to bring God's people into their promised land is on-site prayer. Recall the children of Israel, for instance, circling the city of Jericho.

Across the globe these days, God is stirring ordinary believers to pray persistently while walking their cities street by street. Some of these velvet warriors use prearranged strategies. Others tend to be more spontaneous. Some of these prophetic intercessors make broad appeals, while others pinpoint their petitions like smart bombs for accurate delivery.

Prayer targets vary in distance just like military targets. Some prayer weapons focus on faraway points, way beyond the intercessors' own homes and neighborhoods. Indeed, it is hard to stop at your street, so most of these marching prayer commandos eventually burst into prayers for their entire campus, city or nation. These street warriors are not envisioning a quick fix. Most of these prophetic and priestly intercessors do not imagine themselves to be holding flickering candles against an overwhelming darkness. Rather, they light long fuses in anticipation of major explosions of God's love being set off around the globe. Expectancy seems to expand with every mile.

Some Pointers about On-Site Praying

This is not a new approach to an old concept. It is an ancient strategy with fresh application. Let me clarify the concept of on-site prayer with the following simple points:

1. It is directed intercession: Intercessors paint a target and research the purposes for which the city was founded, major wars or battles fought, destiny declared by the founding fathers, offenses and sins committed, etc.
2. It is intentional prayer for a predetermined period of time.
3. It is exercised in the very places intercessors expect the prayers to be answered.
4. It is prayer with insight. Research and geographical identification are combined with dependence on the Holy Spirit's guidance. Intercessors employ the gifts of the Spirit and seek revelatory insight.
5. It is a refreshment, not a replacement, for normal prayer meetings.

Today, in many of our neighborhoods, you can find signs posted stating, *This Is a Neighborhood Watch Area.* They mean that a particular residential area is watched at night by its citizens. They are looking out for one another. Wouldn't it be great to have a whole city under the watch of the Holy Spirit? As this form of praying on-site with insight grows, maybe we will have entire cities canvassed by prayer walkers. Signs could then be put up that say: *This City Is under Spiritual Surveillance.* Awesome!

May the watchmen come forth, taking their positions on the walls.

Lessons from the Life of Habakkuk

> I will stand on my guard post and station myself on the rampart; and I will keep watch to see what He will speak to me, and how I may reply when I am reproved. Then the LORD answered me and said, "Record the vision and inscribe it on tablets, that the one who reads it may run. For the vision is yet for the appointed time; it hastens toward the goal and it will not fail. Though it tarries, wait for it; for it will certainly come, it will not delay."
>
> Habakkuk 2:1–3

First, we see the watchman go to a quiet place where he can be alone. Second, he quiets himself within by watching for the Lord. Last of all, when God does begin to speak, He says, "Record the vision." Then Habakkuk writes down what he is sensing in his heart.

Practical Suggestions for Journaling

The life of Habakkuk reminds us of the importance of recording what we sense from God. The following ordinary guidelines may make your journaling more successful:

1. Find your own quality time. Avoid times when you are sleepy, fatigued or anxious.
2. Use something practical. A simple spiral notebook is fine. Even a tape recorder can work well.

3. Remember that this is a personal journal. Grammar, neatness and even spelling are not critical issues.
4. Date all entries. State where you were and whom you were with.
5. Include dreams, visions, possible interpretations, personal feelings and emotions in your report.
6. Develop your knowledge of the Bible. *Rhema*, God's immediate word, is tested against the *logos*, the written Word. Include any Scriptures that come to mind.
7. Do not get bogged down with details. This is a summation, not an encyclopedia!
8. Realize that understanding will unfold over time.

Enjoy the journey. This is not intended to be an ordeal. It is just a simple tool to be added to your utility chest.

Walking with Others

As watchmen on the wall, we must be connected with the others in the Body of Christ. We must not be lone rangers shooting at any old thing that shows its head. Although, as you have surmised, I highly value the role of the watchman, I also realize the Holy Spirit speaks to more people than just you and me. Let's walk with the leaders of our cities and submit our impressions to others. Only after receiving confirmation and the green light can we pray effectively to avert the enemy's schemes. "For if the bugle produces an indistinct sound, who will prepare himself for battle?" (1 Corinthians 14:8). We must hear a clear call before jumping into battle.

We need each other. Watchmen need caring pastors. Prophets need the guidance of apostles. Pastors need the exhortation of prophets. Elders need watchmen. When each part does its job, they all work together. But when everyone is doing another's part, nothing gets accomplished.

Although both sit in positions of spiritual authority, there are distinct differences between the watchmen on the walls of a city and the elders who sit at the gates of that city. Prophetic watchmen tune in to what is about to occur and then report to the elders at the gate. The elders then make the decision to open or close the gates of a city or region to the force that the watchmen have foreseen. The watchmen communicate what they see and hear. The city elders, genuine fathers and mothers in the Lord, then discern and act in response.

Don't you think it is about time we cooperate in our cities and regions? For too long the various ministries in our churches have functioned in isolation from and competition with one another. As we have not esteemed and honored the different leadership roles, the Body of Christ has suffered.

We need to trust one another, but trust comes only by relationships and relationships take time. Each of us has to get out of our own little world and into someone else's. When pastors and elders learn to value the intercessory watchmen God has placed in their cities, the enemy will no longer be able to wage successful attacks. And when these prophetic watchmen rid themselves of feelings of neglect and rejection and are cleansed from the spirit of offense, their ministries can be received.

How I long to see the divine cooperation of gatekeepers and watchmen, flowing together in the purposes of God in every city and nation!

The Goal

I yearn for the day the devil will be bound, no longer free to roam the earth. Revelation 20:1–2 portrays this glorious event:

> I saw an angel coming down from heaven, holding the key of the abyss and a great chain in his hand. And he laid hold of the dragon,

the serpent of old, who is the devil and Satan, and bound him for a thousand years.

I have a question for you: What is the chain the angel uses to bind up the serpent, and where did the angel get it? I think this mighty chain is a weapon of spiritual warfare.

Could it be that as our intercession and watching arise to the Lord Most High, He in turn commissions one of His angels to go forth? The angel then takes the great chain of prayer from all of church history and constrains the devil with it. I like to think that the chain in the angel's hand is the great chain of prayer!

As Rick Joyner has stated, "The Lord wants His people to know when He is going to move, when judgment is coming, and when the enemy will come."[2] Oh, may the baton be passed from one watch to another. May the ancient tool of the watch of the Lord, which has been used in generations past, be restored in our day.

With a trumpet placed to my lips, I am releasing a blast calling forth these watchmen. Let's listen, wait and watch to see what the Lord is saying. Let's walk with others and rebuild the walls of protection around our cities. Let's kneel vigilantly on the promises.

And let's remember that all guards need ammunition. Now that we are learning to aim by watching what the enemy is doing, it is time to discharge our weapons. We will discover the bullets of the Word of God that must be loaded into our prayer guns in the next chapter, "Relentless Reminding." So if you are ready, turn to the next chapter, and be prepared to pull the trigger!

Practical Applications—Making It Real!

- Take a weekend prayer retreat.
- Pray in the Spirit and ask Him to show you what the Father is doing right now.

- Establish a watch of the Lord in your church or city with pastors, fivefold ministry leaders and intercessors.
- Establish hours of corporate prayer in your church or ministry.
- Pray corporately on-site with insight in strategic locations to break open a way for the King of glory.
- Record what you hear, feel, see, dream and experience in a journal.

Recommended Reading

The Lost Art of Intercession by James W. Goll (Destiny Image, 1997)
The Watchmen by Tom Hess (Morningstar, 2003)
The Watch of the Lord by Mahesh and Bonnie Chavda (Charisma House, 1999)
The Prophetic Ministry by Rick Joyner (Morningstar, 1997)

7

Relentless Reminding

IF YOU ARE ready to get some ammunition, this chapter is loaded with bullets that will knock out the enemy's artillery. But before we load and shoot, I want to take a moment to clean out the barrel—to make sure we know what we are doing.

Throughout the generations, people have arisen who believe God's Word, the Scriptures, to be true. The holy Scriptures are indeed the infallible, inspired Word of God. I will fight for that just as much as the next guy. The Bible is our standard for doctrine, salvation and moral conduct.

Sincere people may believe in the inerrancy of Scripture yet deny that God's power and spiritual gifts are active today. For many reasons, they believe that acts of supernatural power and the gifts of the Holy Spirit are not necessary or valid for our time. This theological belief system, termed *cessationism*, affirms belief in God and says that His Word is true. Yet for many reasons it often engenders sterile Christianity.

An unbelieving mind that expects nothing may still speak sincerely, but faith is from the heart. Today the Holy Spirit is looking for believing believers.

I have a word for the cessationist: Cessationism is going to cease! God is on the move. He is baring His holy right arm and demonstrating His strength and power and confounding the wise. Just as Jack Deere, a former associate professor of Old Testament at Dallas Theological Seminary, has gone through a paradigm shift and been changed by encounters with a supernatural God, so many others also will be surprised by the voice and power of the Holy Spirit in the days ahead.[1]

A major missing element in the experience of the Word of God is praying the Word back to God. Prayer is the force, you see, that revitalizes and activates God's Word, with the resulting answers—sometimes dramatic ones—actually helping to bring about God's purposes on earth. Awesome!

We must believe God's Word is true, of course. But then we must act on it. So one of the first steps is asking God to do what He wants. It is the ancient art of reminding God of His Word.

Know the Book of Promises

In order to remind God of His Word, we must know it intimately. Get to know your weapon before you use it! This precious Book of promises is as essential to prayer as oxygen and nourishment are to health. Therefore we must be assured absolutely that the Bible is the Word of God.

When I get to heaven, one of the people I want to meet is Andrew Murray—the Dutch Reformed preacher who had a dramatic impact on the nation of South Africa in the nineteenth and early twentieth centuries. The simplicity and piercing quality of his writings have been a guiding light to my own Christian experience.

Let me quote from his famous work *With Christ in the School of Prayer* on the subject of joining the Word and prayer:

"If ye abide in me, and my words abide in you, ask whatsoever ye will, and it shall be done unto you" (John 15:7, KJV). The vital connection between the Word and prayer is one of the simplest and earliest lessons of the Christian life. "I pray—I speak to my Father; I read—my Father speaks to me." Before prayer, God's Word strengthens me by giving my faith its justification and petition. In prayer, God's Word prepares me by revealing what the Father wants me to ask. After prayer, God's Word brings me the answer, for in it the Spirit allows me to hear the Father's voice.

When God reveals Himself in His words, He does indeed give Himself—His love and His life, His will and His power—to those who receive these words, in a reality that surpasses our comprehension. In every promise, He gives us the power to grasp and possess Him. God's Word gives us God Himself.[2]

Isn't this what we are all after? As we become intimately acquainted with the Word of God, we become intimately acquainted with the God of the Word. Then, as we meditate and pray God's Word back to Him, the Holy Spirit enacts the Word we have just prayed.

Isn't God's plan awesome? Just think: He lets us ask Him to do what He wants to do for us. What a mystery and a privilege!

Needed: A Wedding

Christians who believe in the current-day operation of the gifts of the Spirit need to make sure their arsenal includes one of the foundational evangelical truths: the integrity of the Scriptures as the inspired, infallible Word of God and the final authority in salvation, doctrine, conduct, reproof and correction. Many evangelicals, on the other hand, need to add the fervor, faith and power of the present-day ministry of the Holy Spirit. We need a wedding, or fusion, of the school of the Word and the school of the Spirit.

Years ago I heard revivalist statesman Leonard Ravenhill declare, "If you have the Word without the Spirit, you will dry up. If you have the Spirit without the Word, you will blow up. But if you have the

Spirit with the Word, you will grow up." I say amen to this simple declaration.

The Task of Reminding

We saw in the previous chapter that watchmen on the walls are desperately needed today. But what is their task after they have mounted the walls? Yes, they are called to hear what the Lord is saying, but then what? Are there other tasks these prophetic watchmen are to engage in?

We are called to the glorious, laborious—even mundane, at times—task of reminding.

Asking God to Do What He Wants

The primary Scripture, of course, is Isaiah 62:6–7:

On your walls, O Jerusalem, I have appointed watchmen; all day and all night they will never keep silent. *You who remind the LORD*, take no rest for yourselves; and give Him no rest until He establishes and makes Jerusalem a praise in the earth.

emphasis added

What does it mean to "remind the Lord"? Does He have amnesia? Has He forgotten what He said He would do? No, of course not! He has simply determined not to do this task alone. It is the blessed mystery of being a co-laborer with Christ that God is looking for a people on earth who will come into agreement with His plans.

Remember, "If two of you agree on earth about anything that they may ask, it shall be done for them by My Father who is in heaven" (Matthew 18:19). This is not human agreement about what we want God to do. It is an invitation for us to come into agreement with God's plans, pursuits and desires. Then, in agreement with one another *and* with God, we ask (or remind) Him to do what He wishes to do.

Ezekiel 36:37 tells it this way: "Thus says the Lord GOD, 'This also I will let the house of Israel ask Me to do for them: I will increase their men like a flock.'" This passage contains a key, I believe, to the Lord's church growth methodology: What He promises will not come unless we ask Him to do what He wants. I think I can hear the voice of my Master whispering, *I will let you ask Me to do what I want to do!* He declares in Jeremiah 1:12: "I am watching over My word to perform it."

This is the holy, awesome privilege of prophetic intercessors. We are to be relentless reminders who never give up!

The "Until" Clause

Remember, we are to be God's secretary, bringing before our boss the strategic appointments on His prophetic calendar.

"How long are we supposed to do this?" I think you just asked. My answer is simple: I don't know! Isaiah 62 gives us a clue, though. We find a distinctive emphasis in this passage that I call "relentless reminding." Did you notice the word *until*? "Give Him no rest until. . . ." That might be a long time!

The Holy Spirit loves the quality of tenacity. Luke 18:1–8 points this out in the parable of the widow who pleads with the unrighteous judge until she wears him out. Relentless, she just will not take no for an answer! Jesus said of the judge:

"For a while he was unwilling; but afterward he said to himself, 'Even though I do not fear God nor respect man, yet because this widow bothers me, I will give her legal protection, otherwise by continually coming she will wear me out.'"

verses 4–5

Indeed, holy, bold, prevailing prayer often includes an element of divine stubbornness. Like the widow, you will not take no for an answer. I do not know how long you will have to pray before your "until" clause is fulfilled. But I have a word for you: Continue.

Knock on the Wood Table

The "until" clause reminds me of a story I have read and of which I heard firsthand accounts regarding a mighty revival in Argentina in the early 1950s. The story centers on the prayer life of missionary R. E. Miller.[3]

Edward Miller, a missionary from the United States in the early 1950s, had spent years of tireless, zealous activity in Argentina, pastoring churches, holding tent meetings and conducting personal evangelism, with little fruit. It seemed to him that he had tried everything. So, after doing all he could, he decided to try prayer.

He began on his new course of action by praying eight hours a day for revival in his own life and in his community of Mar del Plata. He continued leading Sunday services at his little church but spent most of the rest of the week in intercession before his God.

After six months of waiting on God, searching the Scriptures, fasting and praying, the Lord finally spoke to Edward Miller. It was a simple message: *Continue!*

So he did—relentlessly, as though his very life depended on it.

Months passed. Miller kept the eight-hour watch until God spoke again. This time the Lord told him to announce public prayer meetings that week, which would begin the following Monday night, at the church from 8 P.M. until midnight.

Miller argued with the Lord, telling Him that if he held such a prayer meeting, the only ones to come would be little old ladies, and all they would do was sit and watch him pray.

This did not seem to bother the Lord. He seemed to reply, *I know.*

So Miller announced the meeting. Sure enough, three little old women were the only ones who came. Miller was right about his next objection, too. The ladies just sat and watched him pray for the next four hours. But pray he did.

At the end of the meeting, he asked if anyone had received anything from God. One of the women, the wife of a backslidden man, raised her hand. She described a strange desire to come up and knock on the wood table at the front of the sanctuary. But she felt that would be foolish, so she declined.

Pastor Miller dismissed the meeting and all went home.

The next night the prayer meeting continued. The same three little women came and sat and watched Edward Miller pray—yes, for another four hours. At the close Miller asked the same question, only to get the same response. The meeting closed and they all went home.

They met for the next two nights, with the same results. The woman with the backslidden husband felt compelled again, she said, to come to the front and hit the wood table, and refused to do so.

Frustration began to settle in on Pastor Miller. He had no idea why God would lead her to do that, but how could he get her to comply?

On the last night of the scheduled prayer meeting, the same three women came and sat and watched Brother Miller pray. At the close he asked the same question and received the same response from the same woman.

But this time Miller said, "Sister, we're all going to walk around the table and hit it."

He hoped she would follow them, gather enough courage and knock on the table herself.

Miller passed by and hit the wood table, followed by two of the women. Then the third woman stepped up to the table and knocked on it. When she did, the Holy Spirit swept though the little church and overwhelmed them with glory and a sense of His presence. All three women were baptized in the Spirit and began worshiping God in a language they had not learned.

The news spread and people began to come nightly. Eventually the fire of revival spread to the capital city of Buenos Aires, where tens of thousands gathered in an outdoor sports stadium in 1954, and the Lord saved and healed many under the powerful ministry of Tommy Hicks. It was the beginning of the great Argentine revival of the early 1950s.

Now what was that word Edward Miller heard? *Continue!* As intercessory watchmen on the walls, we need to continue reminding God relentlessly of His Word.

Pleading the Promise

We must still ask the basic question: Of what are we to remind God?

Let's look at two of the most useful bullets we are to load into our gun: the written promises of Scripture and the present-day revelatory promises that have been spoken by the Holy Spirit.

Scriptural Pleas before His Throne

First we are to bring the written promises of Scripture before God's throne. This includes all the promises of God—whether for individuals, families, the Body of Christ, Israel or the nations—and any of the magnificent themes in Scripture. This alone is an immense subject. Praying the Scriptures is a beautiful art that magnifies God and enriches the soul. It is worth the time and investment for your own personal edification, let alone learning a prayer vocabulary and receiving answers.

In the gracious privilege of praying the Scriptures, we are exhorted to come boldly to the throne of God. We are instructed, even commanded to bring strong pleas before our righteous Judge. Glance with me at Isaiah 43:26 from three different translations:

"Put Me in remembrance, let us argue our case together; state your cause, that you may be proved right."

NASB

114

Put me in remembrance: let us plead together: declare thou, that thou mayest be justified.

KJV

Oh, remind me of this promise of forgiveness, for we must talk about your sins. Plead your case for my forgiving you.

TLB

Pleading Your Case Before God

The following are seven ways you can plead your case before God, with a few scriptural examples for each:

1. Plead the honor and glory of God's name (see 2 Samuel 7:26; Psalm 23:3; 31:3; 79:9; 106:8; 109:21; 143:11).
2. Plead God's relationship to you (see Job 10:3, 8–9; 14:15; Psalm 19:14; 33:20; 40:17; 46:1; 63:7; Isaiah 41:14; 54:5, 8; 63:16; 64:8; Malachi 3:17; Romans 8:15).
3. Plead God's attributes (see Deuteronomy 9:18; Nehemiah 9:33; Psalm 4:1; 27:7; 30:10; 86:6, 15–16; 89:1–2; Isaiah 16:5; Daniel 2:18).
4. Plead the sorrows and needs of the people in desperate circumstances (see Psalm 137:1–4; Lamentations 2:20; 5:1).
5. Plead the past answers to prayer (see Psalm 27:9; 71:17–18; 78; 85:1–7; 105; 106; 136).
6. Plead the Word and promises of God (see 1 Chronicles 17:23–26; 2 Chronicles 6:14–17).
7. Plead the blood of Jesus (see Exodus 12:5–23; Romans 5:9; Ephesians 1:7; Colossians 1:20; Hebrews 9:22; 10:19–23; 13:12; 1 John 1:7; Revelation 12:11).

Reminding God of His Word includes presenting your case and detailing your holy arguments before Him. This not only pleases God, but also helps you to understand your need more completely, releases compassion within you, strengthens your holy boldness and arms you with great hunger and desperation.

Revelatory Promises from the Voice of God

The second type of ammunition we are given is the revelatory promises that have been spoken by the Holy Spirit to us as individuals, families, groups, congregations, cities, regions or nations.

Such revelatory promises—hearing the voice of the Lord through personal communion; the *logos* (written Word) becoming a *rhema* (spoken word) in our hearts; visitations from God; the language of dreams and visions; and other biblical means—come from the heart of our heavenly Father through the gifts of the Holy Spirit.

Let us have ears to hear what the Spirit is saying to His Church. Cultivate a culture that values both the God of the Word and the Word of God.

Valuing the Promise

A passage from Paul to Timothy helps us understand our proper response to these revelatory promises:

> This command I entrust to you, Timothy, my son, in accordance with the prophecies previously made concerning you, that by them you fight the good fight, keeping faith and a good conscience, which some have rejected and suffered shipwreck in regard to their faith.
>
> 1 Timothy 1:18–19

First, we see that Paul valued the gift of prophecy. He instructed his son in the faith not just to listen to the previous revelatory words spoken over him, but to "fight the good fight" with them. He seemed to indicate that these prophetic insights were weapons with which to wage war.

Second, Paul told Timothy that these spoken promises were tools to help him stay his course and remain faithful to the Lord and His calling.

And finally, Paul contrasted the ways of others who had suffered shipwreck, and gave Timothy insight to help him avoid this in his own life.

Of course, impressions and revelations must align with the principles of God's Word and be confirmed by brothers and sisters in Christ as authentic. Otherwise we will end up chasing some elusive fantasy and risk becoming (as Paul warned) shipwrecked, having attempted to build our lives on shifting sand.

But once you have secured an authentic prophetic promise, load, take aim and shoot! Fight the fight and wage war with the prophetic.

Fighting with the Revelatory Promise

In Ephesians 6:17 we are told to take "the sword of the Spirit, which is the word of God." The Greek term used here for "word" is *rhema*, a spoken word from God. Revelatory gifts are mighty weapons of warfare. We pray a prophetic promise back to the heart of our Father.

At times, however, after we have done so, we must declare the word to our circumstances and any mountain of opposition standing in the way. We remind ourselves of the promise that lies ahead, and we remind the devil and command any foul spirits—for example, the spirit of discouragement—to back off, declaring what the written and spoken promises of God reveal.

Each of us has purposes, promises and a destiny to find, fight for and fulfill. So take your "Thus saith the Lord" to battle and fight!

This is what I did with my dream that said, *You will have a son and his name will be called Justin.* I spoke that word over Michal Ann's body as well as my own, prayed the dream back to God and waged war with it by telling barrenness and the devil to depart. Believe me, that dream came in handy! Michal Ann and I used our revelatory promise as a megaphone with which to declare life where there was no life. It became a sword of the Spirit in my hand for several years to wield against the onslaught of the enemy.

We have waged war with the revelatory word time and time again. In recent battles, I have loaded my gun with words from another piercing dream that declared, *And your enemies shall become like grasshoppers in your own sight!* God's Word will not return void but will accomplish the very purpose for which it is sent forth. Yes, we win!

Let Faith Arise!

Take any promises that have been spoken to you by the Holy Spirit and turn them into persistent prayer, reminding God of His Word. I say, "Smoke them pistols!" Use these confirmed, authentic words from heaven to create faith within your heart. Let them pave the way for the entrance of ever-increasing faith in your life: "Faith comes from hearing, and hearing by the word of Christ" (Romans 10:17).

Have you heard any words from Jesus lately? Just read the red print in the grand Book and let those words sink deep, deep, deep into your spirit. This supplies something for the wind of God to quicken in your heart. Faith will leap up inside of you, and you will have a divine "knowing" (usually the gift of faith). When that happens, you know that you know that you know. You might not know *how* you know—but you are certain everything is going to be all right!

Remember what the Holy Spirit spoke to Michal Ann when she had yielded her right to have children: *I appreciate your attitude, but I am not requiring this of you. I say to you, you must fight for your children.* So fight we did! In fact, one time I came running out of our bedroom after praying and told my wife, "Now Annie, get your gun!"

Recall the words from Isaiah 62:7: "Give [God] no rest until. . . ." So pray *until*. Michal Ann and I prayed until we finally hit the target.

The Goal

Did you catch the goal of the relentless reminding, which is also stated in Isaiah 62:7? "Give Him no rest until He establishes and makes Jerusalem a praise in the earth." Does this sound intense, strategic or even "end-timey"? You got it. We are invited to labor for the purposes of God to be established in our generation. We are to come into agreement with our Messiah Jesus and echo His prayer: "Your Kingdom come on earth as it is currently being manifested in heaven."

God is not just offering us a place of personal petition. He is calling warrior watchmen to remind Him relentlessly of His predetermined prophetic purpose. This last days outpouring of His Spirit on all flesh will be fulfilled in both the Church and Israel.

There is something so uniquely wonderful in store for Israel and the Church that once you catch a glimpse, you are undone by God's multifaceted wisdom. As it was in Daniel's time and Isaiah's time, so it is coming about again. Watchmen are showing up on the walls and giving God "no rest until He establishes and makes Jerusalem a praise in the earth." (We will take a closer look at this subject in the next chapter, "Israel: God's Prophetic Calendar.")

We declare His promises until His Kingdom has come, until His will is done on earth as it is in heaven. Do not let go of the hem of His garment. Wrestle until . . . !

Now It's Your Turn!

Now it is time to take the bullets and actually load them into your gun. The Lord might allow you a few good practice rounds, but He is delighted when we learn how to take the bullets of Scripture and revelatory gifts and load them into the gun of prayer. Let's proceed, coupling wisdom and faith in relentless reminding, and keep loading and shooting until "the knowledge of the glory of the LORD" fills the earth "as the waters cover the sea" (Habakkuk 2:14).

Before we close this chapter and take a look at Israel, God's prophetic road map, let's turn to Andrew Murray once again. Together let's kneel on the promises by declaring a prayer of dependency from his legendary book *With Christ in the School of Prayer*:

> Blessed Lord! I see why my prayer has not been more believing and effective. I was more occupied with my speaking to You than with Your speaking to me. I did not understand that the secret of faith is this: There can be only as much faith as there is of the living Word dwelling in the soul.
>
> Your Word taught me so clearly to be swift to hear and slow to speak. Lord, teach me that it is only when I take Your Word into my life that my words can be taken into Your heart. Teach me that if Your Word is a living power within me, it will be a living power with You, also. Amen.[4]

In the Kingdom of God, little keys open big doors. Daniel used the keys of study, meditation, prayer, humility, confession and perseverance to unlock the destiny of God for Israel in his generation. Can you do the same? It is your turn. In fact, it is our turn. Let us do so until. . . .

Practical Applications—Making It Real!

- Remind the Holy Spirit to do what He wants to do for us.
- Pray the promises back to God, bringing them to His hearing. Then declare to the powers of darkness that they must step back at the Word of God.
- Bring any promises given through revelation by the Holy Spirit before the Father to remind Him of the not-yet-fulfilled prophetic destiny.

- Take a promise of Scripture devotionally, memorize it and then pray it over your heart for the next week.

Recommended Reading

Intercessors: Discover Your Prayer Power by Tommi Femrite, Elizabeth Alves and Karen Kaufman (Regal, 2000)

Praying the Scriptures: Communicating with God in His Own Words by Judson Cornwall (Creation House, 1990)

The Complete Works of E. M. Bounds on Prayer (Baker, 1990)

8

Israel

God's Prophetic Calendar

I WANT TO TAKE a moment now to share a specific example of the prophetic promises of God coming to pass in our day. This is not a personal testimony or the story of a church or a ministry. It is the story of an entire nation, and the culmination of God's purposes for the entire earth.

The board has been set and the pieces are moving. Throughout the ages, it seems as if God has been waiting for His strategic moment. He is positioning His intercessory knights and prophetic bishops together for a sweeping move—one that all the world will observe closely. No eye will miss the mysterious and fascinating day on God's prophetic calendar when He once again steps into the world of space and time. It is time for the unveiling of the mystery of Israel as the apple of God's eye (see Zechariah 2:8), the crucial piece on God's chessboard.

Although modern Israel is only approaching sixty years old, the Jewish nation is actually one of the oldest on earth. These people and their land reach back to the time of Abraham's prophetic pilgrimage and the covenant promise of God to him and his descendants (see Genesis 17:4–8). After what many considered to be a silence of two thousand years, this land has been reborn. Israel is once again on display before the eyes of the world.

A Brief Overview

How could a remnant of scattered and persecuted Jewish people, who went through their darkest hour in Hitler's Holocaust, suddenly regain their sovereign nation within their ancient territory? Not without divine intervention, for sure, although many Israelis today believe they did it all on their own. Let's take a brief look at the modern history of this region.

On November 29, 1947, the General Assembly of the United Nations adopted a resolution requiring the establishment of a Jewish state in Palestine. The following is a portion of the Proclamation of Independence read by David Ben-Gurion on May 14, 1948:

> The land of Israel was the birthplace of the Jewish people. Here their spiritual, religious and national identity was formed. Here they achieved independence and created a culture of national and universal significance. Here they wrote and gave the Bible to the world. Exiled from the Land of Israel, the Jewish people remained faithful to it in all the countries of their dispersion, never ceasing to pray and hope for their return and the restoration of their national freedom.
>
> Our call goes out to the Jewish people all over the world to rally to our side in the task of immigration and development and to stand by us in the great struggle for the fulfillment of the dream of generations for the redemption of Israel. With trust in Almighty God, we set our hand to this Declaration on the Sabbath eve, the fifth of Iyar, 5708, the fourteenth day of May, 1948.[1]

Just a day later, on May 15, 1948, while this creation had barely come forth, five Arab nations assaulted the newborn state. Egypt, Syria, Jordan, Lebanon and Iraq (forty million Arabs, 1.5 million of them armed) attacked Israel in what became known as the Israeli War of Independence. The war continued for eight months with heavy casualties on all sides. The miracle is that Israel, which had just been reborn, could not be destroyed (see Isaiah 54:17).

A Look behind the Scenes

I wonder what was going on behind the scenes in prayer as the United Nations made this historic decision. Let's part the veil and peer into some prayer history. Rees Howells gave his life to the Lord Jesus and dedicated it to intercession. Few in modern history have changed lives and affected nations with the authority of prayer like this noble Welsh believer. Let us look at this historic time through his eyes.

After the war was over in October and November in 1947, whole days were given to prayer. On eleven different days during those two months, prayer was concentrated on the coming U. N. vote. When on November 27th the news came through that the partition of Palestine had not been carried, the whole Bible College, of which Rees Howells was the founder and principal, gave themselves to intense intercession. In prayer they actually became aware of God's angels influencing the men in the U. N. debate. Before hearing the final outcome they already had full assurance of victory. When on November 29th the news came that the partition proposal had been carried, the College claimed it as one of the greatest days for God in 1900 years![2]

Amazing, isn't it? Prophetic intercessors carry God's heart for Israel!

Disaster Averted

In 1967 the Six-Day War should also have ended in disaster for Israel, but again God's mercy prevailed. Israel not only defeated her enemies, but captured Sinai, the Gaza Strip, the West Bank and the Golan Heights in only six days. They also captured the Jewish quarter of Jerusalem and the remaining Western (Wailing) Wall of the Temple. At this point, the Israelis controlled all holy Jewish and Christian sites.

And consider the outcome of the surprise 1973 Yom Kippur assault. A coalition of Arab nations led by Egypt and Syria and backed by one of the world's two nuclear superpowers, the Soviet Union, attacked on two fronts; but Israel again came back from the brink of defeat to emerge victorious. Attacking Israel by surprise on her holiest day, the Arabs forced the Israelis back and made brief territorial gains. Yet by what I believe was divine intervention, Israel regained all her land. Once again the hand of God, working in part through human beings, protected the outnumbered and despised Jewish nation.

Prophetic Foresight

God's promise to once again gather and protect the nation of Israel is a declaration of His faithfulness and greatness, not Israel's perfection. With this in mind, let's look at some significant Old Testament prophecies regarding Israel's dispersion and regathering.

Jeremiah's Declaration

Jeremiah, the weeping prophet, glimpsed through time and saw that Israel's faithful, covenant-keeping God would once again offer divine protection to His people in the Promised Land:

> Hear the word of the LORD, O nations, and declare in the coastlands afar off, and say, "He who scattered Israel will gather him and keep him as a shepherd keeps his flock."
>
> Jeremiah 31:10

We find three truths contained in this one verse from Jeremiah. First, it was God Himself who scattered Israel from her own homeland. Second, the same God who scattered Israel will regather her to her own land. And third, God will put a divine hedge of protection about her during the process.

Two Regatherings Predicted

With the theme of God's grace and His faithfulness in mind, let's back up and look at the Diaspora (the dispersion) of the Jewish people in history.

The First Regathering

It is my understanding that Scripture tells us the Jews would suffer two major dispersions, or scatterings, followed by two regatherings.

The first scattering occurred in the years when the prophets Daniel and Ezekiel were exiled in the land of Babylon. This was also the period in which the Jews of the Judean kingdom were displaced from their country after Nebuchadnezzar destroyed the Temple, Jerusalem and the commonwealth (see Daniel 1:1–6). Daniel and his associates were kidnapped around 605 BC. The Jews began to return to the land in 538 BC (see 2 Chronicles 36:22–23; Ezra 1:1–4), and the Temple remained flattened until 515 BC (see Ezra 6:15), about seventy years after its destruction.

The prophet Daniel was held captive in Babylon—a foreign land with foreign gods and culture. In about their 63rd year of captivity, while meditating on the Word of God (see Daniel 9:2), Daniel received a revelation from the prophetic promises of Jeremiah:

> " 'This whole land will be a desolation and a horror, and these nations will serve the king of Babylon seventy years. Then it will be when seventy years are completed I will punish the king of Babylon and that nation,' declares the LORD."
>
> Jeremiah 25:11–12

"Thus says the LORD, 'When seventy years have been completed for Babylon, I will visit you and fulfill My good word to you, to bring you back to this place.'"

Jeremiah 29:10

Daniel believed the word and declared it as revealed to Jeremiah—that at the end of seventy years of Babylonian captivity, the children of Israel would be released to return to their own land. Daniel also sought the Lord to reveal any obstacles to the prophetic promise being fulfilled (see Daniel 9:3–19). Daniel then responded to the prophetic word by confessing the sin of his people as his own. The verse that summarizes his confession is Daniel 9:19:

"O Lord, hear! O Lord, forgive! O Lord, listen and take action! For Your own sake, O my God, do not delay, because Your city and Your people are called by Your name."

The fact that Jeremiah spoke accurately and Daniel later knelt on those words is an example of prophetic intercession at its best. God did precisely what His prophets said He would do! At the end of seventy years the Israelites fulfilled the prophecy of their first return to their covenant land. They began to rebuild the walls of Jerusalem.

Israel continued in many more years of faith, sin, repentance, revival and restoration, but the word of the Lord had been fulfilled and God had shown Himself true to His promise.

The Second Regathering

That was not the only dispersion and regathering prophesied by God's watchmen. Isaiah 11:11–12 states that the Lord would set His hand a second time to recover a remnant of His people:

It will happen on that day that the Lord will again recover the second time with His hand the remnant of His people, who will remain, from Assyria, Egypt, Pathros, Cush, Elam, Shinar, Hamath, and from the islands of the sea. And He will lift up a standard for the nations and assemble the banished ones of Israel, and will gather the dispersed of Judah *from the four corners of the earth.*

emphasis added

This Scripture clearly describes a second dispersion and, at some point, a second regathering. The first dispersion did not send these Jews in many directions at once. They remained together—a persecuted yet identifiable people in a foreign nation. But the second scattering would send them to regions beyond the known world of Isaiah's day—to the four corners of the earth. It is my understanding (as well as that of many others) that we are seeing this second great regathering being fulfilled in this generation.

Let's make it simple. The Scriptures explain that there would be a regional dispersion followed by a regional regathering. Then there would be a worldwide dispersion followed by a worldwide regathering. When did the second dispersion occur? It began around AD 70 under the Roman general Titus, when the Jewish people once again fled their homeland and ran for their lives. For approximately nineteen hundred years, they had no political autonomy and were scattered to the four corners of the earth.

Ramon Bennett wrote of this second gathering in his book *When Day and Night Cease*:

> The second gathering began with the trickle of Jews into Palestine after the turn of the last century. The trickle became a stream after 1948 and then a river during the 1950s and 1960s. The river is now in flood stage and in danger of bursting its banks with the masses arriving from the last vestiges of the (former) Soviet Union.[3]

I love it when the purposes of God unfold right in front of our eyes! That is exactly what I see occurring in the Middle East today.

A Divine Appointment

Let me pause for a moment and tell you a true-life story that took place when I returned from my first trip to Israel in 1987. Though this was years ago, I hope you will pick up a little more of God's heart for Israel as I relay this fascinating encounter.

On my return flight from that first trip to Israel, I was mistakenly bumped up to first class. What an accidental blessing—and a divine appointment! I ended up sitting next to a stately gentleman, and my spiritual antennas began buzzing. I knew nothing about him but felt a curious desire to share from the prophetic Scriptures.

"Would you like to know what's next on God's prophetic calendar?" I asked.

He looked at me intently with curiosity. So I began to tell him that Russia and the Eastern European countries would be freed from the grip of Communism and that an exodus of the Jewish people of grand proportions would soon be occurring from the biblical "land of the north." Quoting from Isaiah and Jeremiah, I told him that circumstances in the Middle East would change radically as a result.

Since my neighbor appeared to be listening intently, I continued talking. What would jump out of my mouth next?

Fishermen and Hunters

I took him to Jeremiah 16:14–16, which states:

"Therefore behold, days are coming," declares the LORD, "when it will no longer be said, 'As the LORD lives, who brought up the sons of Israel out of the land of Egypt,' but, 'As the LORD lives, who brought up the sons of Israel from the land of the north and from all the countries where He had banished them.' For I will restore them to their own land which I gave to their fathers. Behold, I am going to send for many fishermen," declares the LORD, "and they will fish for them; and afterwards I will send for many hunters, and they will hunt them from every mountain and every hill and from the clefts of the rocks."

Rarely had I had such an attentive audience! The fellow leaned toward me as if to say, "Is there more?" I plowed ahead, explaining my understanding of these verses, as the Holy Spirit seemed to rest quietly on me.

I began to talk about the terms *fishermen* and *hunters* as stated in Jeremiah, and what they could possibly mean. I told him that the fishermen in Jeremiah were sent out to call the Jewish people to return to their homeland. In fact, one of the first "fishermen" spoke as early as 1897: secular leader Theodor Herzl released an early call at the first World Zionist Congress held in Basil, Switzerland, for the establishment of a Jewish state.

The next major move on the divine chessboard happened in 1917 when General Allenby and the British forces liberated Jerusalem from four hundred years of Turkish domination. They signed the Balfour Declaration calling for a national home for the Jews.

I went on to explain that in 1933 Zeb Jabotinsky, one of the early Jewish pioneers in Palestine, warned the Jews of Germany: "There is no future for you here. Come back to your land while the doors are still open."[4]

The times changed at that point, from the fishermen of mercy to the hunters of judgment. What followed eventually led to the slaughter of six million Jews.

God's Great Treasure

After hearing about the fishermen and hunters, the gentleman seated next to me pulled out his notebook, took a few notes. Then he closed his pad and began to probe gently, asking who I was, what I was doing on this trip and whether I had talked with any international military leaders.

I realized I had struck a nerve, but had no idea that this was a man of tremendous influence and responsibility. In fact, this man turned out to be the deputy secretary of the Joint Chiefs of Staff in

President Reagan's administration, in charge of military strategy in the Middle East.

I must admit, it was kind of exciting! I guess the Lord wanted him to know what was coming next. As I shared from the Scriptures with him, I knew some of God's great treasure was being placed into his heart.

My own appetite was whetted for more divine appointments! May He lead each of us into opportunities to draw people's attention to Israel.

More about the Second Regathering

Back to our main topic: Jeremiah. Let's look in more depth at what the prophetic Scriptures say about the second regathering. Jeremiah's trumpet sends out a clarion call:

> "Behold, I am bringing them from the north country, and I will gather them from the remote parts of the earth, among them the blind and the lame, the woman with child and she who is in labor with child, together; a great company, they will return here. With weeping they will come, and by supplication I will lead them; I will make them walk by streams of waters, on a straight path in which they will not stumble; for I am a father to Israel, and Ephraim is My firstborn."
>
> Hear the word of the LORD, O nations, and declare in the coastlands afar off, and say, "He who scattered Israel will gather him and keep him as a shepherd keeps his flock."
>
> Jeremiah 31:8–10

These verses specifically mention "the north country" as one of the primary places of exodus and returning. To understand the regions involved, we must look at the map. It is interesting to note that Moscow is located directly north of Israel.

Jeremiah explained more about how God's people would be led out: "With weeping they will come, and by supplication I will lead them" (verse 9). What is supplication? *Strong's Concordance* renders the meaning of this word simply as "strong prayer." Awesome! Once again we are given the secret of the fulfillment of the prophetic promise: the desperate prayer of the heart (weeping) and praying the promise back to God (supplication).

Here again we find God's purposes birthed through prophetic intercession. I was privileged to later participate with Jonathan Bernis in several of his outreaches in the former Soviet Union where we saw thousands of Russian Jews give their hearts to Yeshua as their Messiah. History was continuing to unfold as intercessors paved the way for prophetic fulfillment.

Let me share another vivid testimony that will drive this point home.

A Contemporary Fulfillment

Earlier I mentioned my dear friend from the Czech Republic, Moravian pastor Evald Rucky. In early spring of 1991, you recall, he became ill from a heart condition while ministering in Sweden and was taken to the hospital. His doctors said he had fallen into a coma. But as Evald understands it, the Lord let him escape to heaven for a while to enjoy His presence before being called back by his best friend's tears.

While Evald was caught up in the Lord's presence, he experienced many things and saw a few events before they actually transpired on earth. At one point he saw a white bridge that rose up out of Ethiopia, reached through the clouds and came down into Israel. As Evald watched, some fifteen thousand dark Ethiopian people crossed over the bridge into Israel.

"What is this?" Evald asked the Lord.

The Holy Spirit answered him, *Oh, these are My ancient Jewish people that I will bring home from Ethiopia to Israel.*

Evald inquired further: "How does this come to pass?"

Again an answer came: *Why, this, too, happens in answer to the prayers of the saints.*

What a sight and what an explanation! But what was it that Evald actually saw?

In May 1991, just a few weeks later, Operation Solomon made history. The headline of the June 1, 1991, *Jerusalem Post* read, "Operation Solomon Flies 14,400 to Israel in 24 Hours: Ethiopian Jewry Rescued." The article went on to state:

> Israel made history Saturday completing a massive airlift of some 14,000 beleaguered Ethiopian Jews from the Addis Ababa to their ancestral homeland in a breathtaking 24 hours. Operation Solomon, conducted by the IDF and in coordination with the Jewish Agency, foreign ministry and other bodies, as well as the Ethiopian government, brought tears to many of the thousands of the Israelis who took part in a reunification of the Ethiopian Jews with their 20,000 family members already in Israel.[5]

Now let me quote to you from an Associated Press news release concerning the same historic event. The tone of the *News Messenger's* article sounded a lot like Scripture. The bold headlines declared, "Israel Rescues 15,000," and the subhead, "Massive Airlift Transports Ethiopian Jews to Safety." Now for the amazing article:

> Israel brought 15,000 Ethiopian Jews to their promised land, plucking them out of the besieged Addis Ababa in a dramatic two-day airlift that ended Saturday. Operation Solomon's 40 flights brought virtually all of the Ethiopian known Jews held to be the descendants of one of the lost ten tribes of Israel to their new lives in the Jewish state. The airlift, the largest such evacuation that Israel has ever mounted, was reminiscent of the Biblical exodus. The newcomers walked, hobbled and were carried down the gangways. Many were clad in flowing robes with only the humble possessions they could carry. One old woman knelt and kissed the tarmac. Four babies were born aboard the flights. "This is a very moving experience," said one of the pilots. "It's not every day one gets to play a part of making history."[6]

Old news at this point, you say? Sounds to me like prophecy of Scripture being fulfilled! In the rapidly developing events of our day, let's not forget the exploits God has already done to fulfill His unchanging Word.

In the meantime, remember the question my friend Evald asked of his heavenly guide: "How does this come to pass?" In the answer, *Why, this, too, happens in answer to the prayers of the saints,* we once again see prophetic intercession giving birth to the promises of God. How does it work? God's pure prophetic promise, whether in Scripture or by the authentic release of the gifts of the Spirit, is knelt upon in humble, persistent prayer by believers in Christ—and answers come tumbling forth!

Proclaim, Praise and Pray

Little keys open big doors—remember? Then what are the keys needed to unlock the promises of God? Jeremiah 31:7 perhaps summarizes better than any other verse the believer's practical response to God's prophetic invitation:

> Thus says the LORD, "Sing aloud with gladness for Jacob, and shout among the chief of the nations; proclaim, give praise and say, 'O LORD, save Your people, the remnant of Israel.'"

This verse points out three important and distinct actions. They are the words *proclaim, praise* and *say.* The word *say* in this context refers to prayer, since we are exhorted through "saying" to talk to God. God gives us three successive keys to insert into the prison door on behalf of the Jewish people, to help deliver them into God's destiny. These keys are *the power of proclamation, the power of praise* and *the power of prayer.*

Michal Ann and I now carry a tremendous burden for Israel as prophetic intercessors. In fact, we are now launching the Israel Prayer

Coalition as another phase of this burden. (Visit www.israelprayer coalition.com for details.) Most everything we do on behalf of Israel is connected to one of these three simple activities: proclaiming God's Word, praising His holy name and praying.

Like Elijah I have called for the drought to end and for a time of mercy to begin. I have prayed for the peace of Jerusalem. I have been awakened in the middle of the night just to sit, wait and listen to the voice of God concerning His purposes for the Jewish people. I have been called into active service, alert in the night watches during times of war.

Let the Holy Spirit tune your heart to heaven right now. May *Elohim*, the Creator and Supreme Being, give you the spirit of wisdom and revelation concerning His prophetic calendar for Israel, and may His heart for Jerusalem beat in your own as we help give birth to God's purposes through prophetic intercession.

Practical Applications—Making It Real!

- Take several of the Scriptures from Isaiah and Jeremiah relating to Israel's future and pray them back to the Father, asking Him to bring forth His Word.

- Wait on the Lord and ask Him to shine His light in your heart to expose any areas of anti-Semitism or false teaching regarding Israel and the Jews. Bring these before the Lord in confession and repentance.

- Meditate on the list of promises and appointments in God's prophetic calendar for Israel, letting them sink into your heart. Then plunge into prophetic intercession for God's people.

- Save your money and plan to participate in one of many prayer journeys to Israel, praying the promises on-site with insight.

Recommended Reading

When Day and Night Cease: A Prophetic Study of World Events and How Prophecy Concerning Israel Affects the Church and You by Ramon Bennett (Arm of Salvation, 1993)

Promised Land: The Future of Israel Revealed in Prophecy by Derek Prince (Chosen, 2005)

Your People Shall Be My People by Don Finto (Regal, 2001)

Praying for Israel's Destiny: Effective Intercession for God's Purposes in the Middle East by James W. Goll (Chosen, 2005)

PART 3

A Heart for Prophetic
Intercession

9

The Lost Art
of Prophetic Intercession

THE GREAT SERPENT has coiled himself around the globe, and who shall set the world free from him?"[1] This was the message from the "prince of preachers," Charles Spurgeon.

If the serpent had a strong grip in Spurgeon's day, what can be said about our own? Is the grip of the enemy the reason a new breed of radical, fierce, yet humble and broken intercessors is emerging on the scene? Remember Psalm 24:1: "The earth is the LORD's, and all it contains." We are seeing a joining of the offices of priest and prophet. After years of the serpent's hold, it is time for a company of anointed prophetic intercessors to lay hold of God's promises for our generation.

A Widow Called Anna

One of the most significant yet little-known characters in the New Testament is the prophetess Anna. After seven years of married life, she was suddenly widowed. We do not know how she lost her husband, if she had children or whether she was left all alone. All we are told is that this sacrificial woman, now age 84, extravagantly devoted the rest of her years to the ministry of prayer and fasting, waiting in the Temple for the coming of the Messiah.

> There was a prophetess, Anna the daughter of Phanuel, of the tribe of Asher. She was advanced in years and had lived with her husband seven years after her marriage, and then as a widow to the age of eighty-four. She never left the temple, serving night and day with fastings and prayers.
>
> Luke 2:36–37

We do not know the age at which Anna married. In all likelihood she was young, possibly seventeen or even younger. If so, she was widowed at least by the age of 24 and then devoted the next sixty years of her life to priestly intercession. In the event that she married a little later in life, let's say at 37, she would still have been widowed at 44 and have spent forty years waiting on God. Or say she got married late in life, at 67. By the time her husband departed, she was the ripe old age of 74. That would mean she had spent ten years in the Temple.

Whew! Whether it was ten years or forty or sixty, she had been at the Temple for a long time, crying out to the Lord day and night with prayer and fasting. Anna must have been consumed with a burning passion those long years. After years of what some would call inactivity her waiting paid off.

Like you, I have seen numerous prayer ministries start but few continue. It takes a prophetic vision to continue such a ministry long-term. You need a clear revelation of your target, purpose and goal. Prayer ministries that endure over a period of years, I have found, are those fueled by inspiration. But what inspires them? Burdens and crises come and go. What motivates intercessors or intercessory groups over the long haul?

Only one thing. Like the praying prophetess Anna—and like David, the shepherd-king—we must have a consuming vision of the One we serve. First and foremost we need a vision of our Lord Himself. After all, He is the goal and prize of life.

What Was Her Prophetic Ministry?

In what way can Anna be considered a prophetess? The Scripture does not tell us that she wore a coat of camel's hair or ate locusts and wild honey. I doubt that she pointed a long, snarling finger at people and said brazenly, "Thus saith the Lord!" revealing the secret sins of their hearts. We have no clue that she ever confronted the prophets of Baal like Elijah of old or called down fire from heaven. In fact, we find not even one recorded prophecy from this devout woman.

If she did not give personal prophetic words, then what was her prophetic ministry? She was a woman of the secret place, not with a public ministry at all but interceding with the purposes of God for her generation. The expression of her prophetic ministry was her enduring intercession. She was a prophetic, intercessory Jesus fanatic!

When Joseph and Mary brought eight-day-old Jesus to the Temple to present Him to the Lord,

> At that very moment [Anna] came up and began giving thanks to God, and continued to speak of Him to all those who were looking for the redemption of Jerusalem.
>
> Luke 2:38

Undoubtedly Anna's intercessory burden had included searching through the prophetic promises that had not yet been fulfilled. This verse in Luke tells us that she "continued to speak of [Jesus] to all those who were looking for the redemption of Jerusalem." You see, Anna was looking for a Deliverer, the Messiah, the hope of Israel. She was one of a special task force of prophetic intercessors whom

God had ordained for that generation. They were the ones who were listening and watching for the Lord's appearing. Like Joshua they were waiting at the doorway of the tent of meeting in hopes that they would be the first to see the Lord's great presence. Anna was doubtless praying through those beloved prophetic promises of a coming Messiah.

Wanted: Holy Ghost PUSHers!

The Lord is searching for an "Anna Company" in our day, intercessors who will pray through the promises of the Second Coming of our lovely Lord and Messiah. Who will pave the way for the coming of the Lord? New recruits are wanted and the Holy Spirit is sending out invitations today. Have you responded yet?

Many of the greatest intercessors of our time have been women. Their sensitivity of spirit, their passion for the things of God, the readiness with which they yield their hearts to Him to plead His cause—all these characteristics serve intercessors well. It was a woman who anointed Christ for burial. Women remained at the cross when the rest of the disciples fled. Women were the first to proclaim, "He is risen!"

The real issue, of course, is not whether you are male or female. To be part of this "Anna Company," all you need is an ever-growing conviction of the purposes of God and a desire to pray through God's promises until you see them fulfilled. These revelatory warriors know how to PUSH—*Pray Until Something Happens!*

In our day and time the Holy Spirit is drawing together a people who will stand united in a congregation, city or region. God is wooing believers to one another as covenant prayer partners. He is summoning the leaders in an area to stand together and fight. He is calling all of us in His Body to join hands and take our places until the promises of a great, end-time visitation for our generation have come to pass.

Let us arise, O Church, put off our slumber and cry out until we, like Anna two thousand years ago, behold Christ. It is time for a bunch of Holy Ghost PUSHers to show up on the scene.

Defining Our Terms

Let's summarize a few thoughts on the *priest*, the *prophet* and the task of *prophetic intercession* before we dive off the board into the deep end of the pool.

The job of the *priest* is to plead the needs of the people before the Lord. He does not represent himself, but carries the burdens, needs and cares of others before our majestic God. As priests our hearts pulse with the needs of our cities, congregations and nations. As New Testament priests, we represent others to God.

What is the job of the *prophet*? He represents the interests of God to the people. Having stood in the council of the Almighty, the prophet releases what is in His heart through a clarion call. The prophet releases words, thoughts, messages and inspirations that are beating in the heart of God right now.

What is *prophetic intercession*? It is the place where the ministry of the priest and prophet unite. A passage in Jeremiah says it wonderfully: "If they are prophets, and if the word of the LORD is with them, let them now entreat the LORD of hosts" (Jeremiah 27:18). Prophetic intercessors do not only pronounce the word of the Lord; they in turn pray the promise back to the Father! In so doing they actually give birth to the promise.

Prophetic intercession, therefore, paves the way for the fulfillment of the prophetic promise.

How Does Prophetic Intercession Work?

In prophetic intercession the Spirit of God pleads the covenant promises made throughout history to be enacted in our day. This inspired form of intercession is the urge to pray, given by the Holy Spirit, for a situation or circumstance about which you may have little natural knowledge. But you are praying the prayer request that is on the heart of God. He nudges you to pray so that He can intervene. The Holy Spirit Himself directs you to pray in a divine manner to bring forth His will on earth as it already is in heaven.

"Now say that again?" you are asking.

Prophetic intercession is the ability to receive a prayer request from God and pray it back to Him. God's hand comes on you, and He imparts His burden to you. Prophetic intercession is not as much *praying to God* as it is *praying with God*! Oh my! What a difference! We then stand in the gap in God-inspired, God-directed intercession.

We do not take "promise boxes" or one of those plastic loaves of bread with Bible verses inside and randomly select a verse to pray through. No, we combine waiting, listening and reading the Scriptures with letting the Holy Spirit remind us of the promise that is on His heart at that moment. We let God's heartbeat pulse in our own beings. Isn't that exciting?

Any message—whether it is preached truth, prayed burden or spontaneous utterance—is prophetic only if it comes from God and brings people into the knowledge of God. Prophetic intercession pleads for the maturity of the Body of Christ—that the society of redeemed mankind would expand to the ends of the earth. It is the place where the priest and prophet unite, calling "for the earth [to] be filled with the knowledge of the glory of the LORD, as the waters cover the sea" (Habakkuk 2:14).

Prophetic intercession does not always take place in a prayer room. As a believer receives a burden from the Lord, which can happen anyplace at all, he or she responds by expressing this back to Him. Sometimes this is accompanied by, or followed by, distinct actions before God, others and the world, as well as appropriate declarations to block hosts of darkness from their diabolical aspirations. Awesome!

"To Breathe Together"

Ours is the privilege of entering into the actual intercession of Christ, yielding ourselves to Him so that He can flow through us. In prayer we become laborers with Christ and enter into partnership with the Creator of the universe!

The burden of prophetic intercession begins as a flame and grows into a consuming fire as the revelation concerning the purposes of God for our generation increases. It might start as an inner conviction of His will, a sudden awareness of His nearness or hearing of a situation that triggers a spiritual response.

All prophetic intercession carries the struggle of birth. The heart of the intercessor becomes the womb in which God's prophetic purposes come forth. In this place the struggle between old traditions and new ways takes place. We become the handmaidens of the Lord in whom the "new and old wineskins" collide. As we hear God's voice, we become convinced that a radical revolution of the Christian faith is near. The prophetic intercessor conspires with God that His glory will be seen, felt and known in the earth.

The word *conspire* means literally "to breathe together." It expresses the most intimate joining of life. When God created man from the dust of the earth, He "breathed into his nostrils the breath of life; and man became a living being" (Genesis 2:7). This Hebrew word translated *breathed* can mean "to breathe violently." Such was the occasion when there was the sound of a violent wind filling the Upper Room as God sent His Spirit upon and into His newborn Church.

Prophetic intercession is our conspiring together with God, "breathing violently" into situations through prayer to bring forth life. When God's people receive the spirit of grace and supplication (see Zechariah 12:10), they share a sense of divine possibility and excitement. God shatters their old expectations.

Prayer embraces new horizons, challenges and possibilities. It liberates intercessors from their limited human perspective. As Ephesians 2:6 tells us, we have been "raised . . . up with [Christ], and seated . . . with Him in the heavenly places." These focused warriors now look from a heavenly vantage point. They see with the discerning eyes of the Holy Spirit. Their intercession assumes a revelatory dimension. As they gather up the promises God has willed for their day and age, they stake claim to them tenaciously in the judicial courts of heaven.

"This all sounds great, James," you are saying. "But can you help to drive the point home?"

I would be glad to. Let me share another treasure from my war chest.

Waging Prophetic Warfare

History was written when we prayed! There we were, spending hours together interceding in the Ukrainian Pentecostal Church in lower Manhattan where fellow prophetic intercessor Richard Glickstein pastored a Sunday evening congregation called One Accord. Under the mandate of our senior statesman, Dick Simmons, this small group of prophetic intercessors was calling on God early one morning in the fall of 1987 for mercy on our nation.

We came together from different parts of the United States— Richard from New York City; Dick from Bellingham, Washington; David Fitzpatrick, a passionate, focused pastor then from Michigan; Kevin Nolker, an elder from the church I formerly pastored in Warrensburg, Missouri; and, of course, myself.

Much like today, our nation was embroiled in a hair-raising conflict in the Persian Gulf. Iran and Iraq had been at war for a decade, and it was spilling over into the entire region. Oil was the precious commodity that the United States needed, but the Gulf, which American ships traversed, had been laid with explosive mines. It was an intense time, with President Ronald Reagan squaring off with the Iranian Shiite head of state, Ayatollah Ruholla Khomeini. This was the setting in which the Lord had led us to intercede.

Under Dick's leadership we met at 5 A.M. on September 23, 1987, to call on the name of the Lord. Different groups of people came and went that early morning until around ten o' clock, as we sought the face of God.

A Map of the Middle East

I was sprawled out on the floor under the front pew of the sanctuary for those five hours, somewhat hidden away. I prayed quietly the entire time using the gift of tongues (see 1 Corinthians 12:10; 14:1–4, 15–16; Jude 20). While praying in the Spirit, I kept seeing in my mind's eye a picture of a map of the Middle East. I would pray and watch, watch and pray, trying to get a clearer view of this map and an understanding of what to do with what I was seeing.

As I lay on the floor, praying in tongues and seeing the map, "knowings" were coming to me. I had the conviction that I was glimpsing a critical circumstance. As I kept peering at the map, I saw something that looked like a tiny island nation. I could see letters spelling out B-a-h-r-a-i and then a final letter. I could not tell if it was an *n* or an *m*. But it would not go away! I sensed in the Holy Spirit that there was a U.S. military presence in this tiny nation, which was unknown to me in those pre–Gulf War days. I also knew that Iran, under the influence of the prince of Persia (mentioned in Daniel 10:13), was about to release an unprovoked attack against the United States on this island that could catapult the world into World War III before God's appointed time.

A heavy thought! But it would not go away.

So I prayed, I watched and I listened to the others intercede. The picture and impressions would not leave.

As our time of intercession was winding to a close, I stood to my feet and said sheepishly, "Hey, guys, I have something to share." I went ahead and told them what I just told you. Then I asked for their counsel and suggested that we pray.

They responded, to my great comfort, "First of all, we don't even know if such a place exists. Secondly, if it does, we don't know if the U.S. has a military presence there. But we do have a history with you and we trust you. So let's pray and see what happens."

And we did.

Clothed with Supernatural Authority

There we were, on a Holy Ghost hunt-and-search party! But it was no party; it was serious business. I was pacing the floor and ended up on the platform standing behind the podium. The brothers followed me there and laid their hands on me.

At once I was clothed with supernatural authority, and a missile of declaration shot out of my mouth. I was as astonished as anyone at what came forth! For about fifteen seconds I was clothed with power—long enough for the Holy Spirit to launch from our midst a weapon of prophetic warfare.

I shouted, "I command the prince of Persia, which is coming against the U.S. military presence on the tiny nation of B-a-h-r-a-i-something, to be bound, in Jesus' name!"

That was it. But something happened. We all knew it.

Then, just as quickly as that supernatural authority came, it also lifted. We all looked at one another and decided to do something really spiritual—go get something to eat! But as we exited the church about ten o'clock and headed to our favorite Russian restaurant in lower Manhattan for a late breakfast, I couldn't stand it.

"I have to find a library or something," I told my buddies, "and see if such a place called B-a-h-r-a-i-something exists."

New York University was right across the street, but I kept walking with my friends. Then, to my great delight, we happened on a newsstand. There, sitting on the rack, was a strange-looking newspaper, peach in color. The front-page headline read, "Tehran Threatens to Retaliate against U.S. for Ship Attack." In the middle of the page the subheadline stated, "American Navy in Second Confrontation."

Then it showed a map of the Middle East and spoke of the U.S. Naval Command in a place called Bahrain, an archipelago of islands in the Persian Gulf.

There it was, right in front of my eyes! Captivated, I bought a copy of the paper, called the *Financial Times*, a European business newspaper. (I still have it to this day.) Although no American newspaper that I ever saw carried this report, the lead story of the *Financial Times*, dated September 23, 1987, reads:

> In a lengthy address to the U.N. General Assembly on the seventh anniversary of the start of the Gulf war, [Iranian head of state] Khomeini repeatedly denounced the U.N. and the U.N. Security Council in the bitterest of terms. Departing from his prepared text he said, "I want to draw urgent attention to the very grave and immediate danger provoked by the U.S. Administration's latest action which is very dangerous to the whole world. . . . This is a beginning for a series of events, the bitter consequences of which shall not be confined to the Persian Gulf, and the U.S. as the initiator shall bear responsibility for all ensuing events. I declare here that the U.S. shall receive a proper response for this evil act."[2]

Needless to say, I heaved a sigh of relief when I saw this report. Bahrain indeed existed, and God had been directing our praying to avert an escalation of the crisis. The good news is, nothing happened! No retaliation ever occurred. In fact, after this point the conflict began to unravel.

Coincidence? Maybe. We will never know for sure this side of heaven. But I think when the history books of heaven are opened up, we will see that the Holy Spirit was landing on many prophetic intercessors that day across the global Body of Christ, urging them to pray what was on the heart of God.

Dramatic? You bet! God is waiting on us to take our places before Him—to get in His face!—and then to pray back through intercession the promise of divine intervention.

A Prophetic Appeal for Intercession

In closing this chapter, I would like to present to you a portion of a relevant prophetic word given by one of the Church statesmen of our day, Jack Hayford, chancellor of King's College and former senior pastor of Church On The Way in Van Nuys, California. Although the word was delivered August 1, 1980, it is yet one of the clearest trumpet sounds I have ever heard and worthy of our review.[3]

Read and listen with your heart and see if you do not agree. This word needs to be sounded once again, I believe, in this decade:

The Lord God would call all of His redeemed in this land to lift up their eyes and look! Over your nation there are leaden skies, clouds of impending judgment which hang heavy with a rain of fury and indignation which this people have brought upon themselves. As sin has risen as a vapor of evil, now clouds of judgment have formed and shall shortly be precipitated in wrath and destruction, except an intercessor rise to hold back the storm.

And so the Lord calls: O Church, cause your words to rise in prayers of intercession unto deliverance. The skies are dropping lower, skies of lead weighted with judgment, but your entry with prayer can save the day. For the Lord would have you see that your intercession, O Church, rises like pillars, extending through prayer and pressing back the impending judgment, pushing the leaden skies upward and backward. Take your place as pillars of prayer, for I would that there be mercy upon this nation rather than judgment; I would there be healing rather than death!

Cause the word to go forth with understanding that My people need not surrender to the storm which threatens. Did I not deliver Nineveh when repentance came? If you pray ceaselessly until the leaden skies of judgment be lifted by pillars of prayer, then will the light, the glory and the blessing of the Lord flood your land and healing come again. Lift up your voices with praise, raising pillars of intercession, and you shall see the deliverance of God, if you will pray as He directs.

Where Are My Daniels and Esthers?

Some years ago I took a train from Heidelberg to Rosenheim, Germany—a six-hour excursion in the middle of the night. While attempting to rest on the train, I kept hearing the gentle voice of the Holy Spirit. I know He was talking to me as an individual, but He was also imparting a burden for a band of people to come forth.

Here is what I heard Him speak:

Where are My Daniels? Where are My Esthers? Where are My Deborahs? And where are My Josephs?

Repeatedly I heard His piercing, relentless plea:

Where are My Daniels? Where are My Esthers? Where are My Deborahs? And where are My Josephs?

I close out this strategic chapter, then, with this plea. I am convinced that you, reading this book right now, were created "for such a time as this" (Esther 4:14). For such a prophetic intercessory task, God brought *you* forth. Will you arise and be one of His radical revolutionaries? Will you be one of the answers to His persistent plea?

You remember the vision I saw, described in the opening chapter, of the velvet warriors moving forward on their knees. Many vacancies exist; you can still sign up. It is not too late to answer the call, volunteer for on-the-job training and be commissioned as one of God's servant-warriors. I think I can hear drumbeats in the background. The march is beginning. Yes, humble, persistent warriors are aligning themselves under God's command. In fact, I think I can hear another sound coming forth: "Calling all watchmen! The time has come for you to mount your walls." Let's restore the lost art of prophetic intercession.

Who will answer the call? Will you join me in making history?

Practical Applications—Making It Real!

- Pray His coming promises. The Lord is searching for an "Anna Company" that will pray through prophetic promises of the coming Messiah until He comes.

153

- Ask the Holy Spirit to direct you to a covenant prayer partner.
- Pastors, join together for the task of intercession for your city.
- Wait before God to hear or receive His burden, and then respond back to the Lord.

Recommended Reading

Intercessory Prayer: How God Can Use Your Prayers to Move Heaven and Earth by Dutch Sheets (Regal, 1997)
Possessing the Gates of the Enemy by Cindy Jacobs (Chosen, 1991)
Prophetic Intercession by Barbara Wentroble (Regal, 2000)
This Day We Fight! Breaking the Bondage of a Passive Spirit by Francis Frangipane (Chosen, 2005)

10

Crisis Intercession

*W*HERE ARE MY *Daniels? Where are My Esthers? Where are My Deborahs? And where are My Josephs?* These words that echoed in my being as I rode that train in Germany have stuck with me. There was a pleading, a haunting urgency in His voice that night.

What is the Holy Spirit searching for? For those with "an extraordinary spirit" like Daniel (Daniel 6:3) to whom He can give understanding of the end times. He is scouring the earth to find those prophetic watchmen who arise like Esther "for such a time as this" (Esther 4:14). He searches for Deborahs (see Judges 4:4–5) to emerge from their comfort zones, making a difference in every area of society. And He is looking for Josephs, wise interpreters of dreams who can save their people from catastrophe (see Genesis 41:56–57).

Where are these courageous men and women of God for this generation? Where are the Praying Hydes of our day who will win souls in prayer and then one by one in daily life?

I am convinced that to live victoriously in the hours ahead, we must have the anointing of intercession like these champions who have gone before us. Perilous times lie ahead as the last days unfold (see 2 Timothy 3:1). Times even more perilous than World War II. We need a new generation of revolutionaries who will walk in the anointing—like the Welsh intercessor Rees Howells, whose prayers launched from the Swansea Bible College, along with those of his students and faculty, saved Great Britain from the invasion of the Nazis in World War II.

From the Life of Rees Howells

Rees Howells's burden consumed him for world evangelism, the nation of Israel and the defeat of God's enemies. On the very day that Britain declared war, Howells proclaimed firmly,

> The Lord has made known to us that He is going to destroy Hitler and the Nazi regime, that the world may know that it was God and God alone who has scattered the dictators. Three and a half years ago the College prayed this prayer for weeks and months and we firmly believe He will now answer it.[1]

Did you catch the wording? This was the prophetic in full operation (*the Lord has made it known to us*) toward the purpose of crisis intervention (*going to destroy Hitler and the Nazi regime*) through the vehicle of intercession (*we prayed this prayer for weeks and months*). Mercy! Do you think we still have some things to learn?

Let's continue looking at the pages of this crisis intercessor.

> From this time on, through all the years of the war the whole College was in prayer every evening from seven o' clock to midnight with only a brief interval for supper. They never missed a day. This was in addition to an hour's prayer meeting every morning, and very often at midday. There were many special periods when every day was given up wholly to prayer and fasting.[2]

As the Nazis marched across Europe, the college stood firm before God!

On September 14, 1940, with full conviction from God, Howells recorded a triumphant message in his journal. "Because we have believed, God has made known to us what is to come to pass. Every creature is to hear the gospel; Palestine is to be regained by the Jews; and the Savior is to return."[3]

After the war was over, Air Chief Marshall Lord Dowding made the following observation about the Battle of Britain:

> Even during the battle one realized from day to day how much external support was coming in. At the end of the battle one had the sort of feeling that there had been some special Divine intervention to alter some sequence of events which would otherwise have occurred.[4]

Raise them up once again, Lord—these prophetic intercessors— whose hearts carry God's heart for world evangelism, God's purposes for the Jewish people and crisis intercession! Indeed, Rees Howells's bold cries of crisis intercession released heaven's intervention.

Let's continue in our study of crisis intercession by examining the life of one of my favorite Old Testament prophets. Let's learn the lesson that mercy triumphs over judgment from this tough yet tender warrior of the Lord—the prophet Amos.

Revealing, Repenting and Relenting

Amos was a shepherd and farmer. He came from Tekoa, a small village six miles south of Bethlehem. Although he was a native of Judah, his mission was to the northern kingdom. And even though he had not been trained in the prophetic schools, the Lord called Amos out from his flock, saying, "Go, prophesy unto my people Israel" (Amos 7:15, KJV).

This country boy saw through the veneer of temporal prosperity and exposed the inherent weakness and decay in Israel that was inviting doom. Righteousness—Amos' dominant theme—was necessary for the security of the nation and for the stability of her faith. Where righteousness was lacking, no amount of ritual would ever avert judgment.

The Locust Swarm

The Lord GOD showed me, and behold, He was forming a locust-swarm when the spring crop began to sprout. And behold, the spring crop was after the king's mowing. And it came about, when it had finished eating the vegetation of the land, that I said, "Lord GOD, please pardon! How can Jacob stand, for he is small?" The LORD changed His mind about this. "It shall not be," said the LORD.

Amos 7:1–3

Through visionary revelation, the Lord warned Amos of coming devastation to the vegetation by a swarm of locusts. Amos responded to this prophetic warning through immediate, bold intercession, appealing to God's mercy: "Lord GOD, please pardon!" (verse 2).

The vision appeared to Amos alone, and he alone interceded. Perhaps this was because he understood the relationship between responsibility and authority. Amos, a farmer by trade, received the revelation of the destruction of the crops. This judgment that would have decimated the people of God also struck a personal note. And from his place of responsibility he was granted authority through prayer. Amos cried out to God for pardon for his people. He acknowledged that they deserved the judgments but pleaded for God to relent.

After his cry of repentance, Amos reminded the Lord of the condition of "Jacob," referring to Israel, the northern kingdom: "How can Jacob stand, for he is small?" (verse 2). Here Amos reminded the Lord that those people bore His covenant name in the earth, despite their wickedness. He pleaded on the basis of God's reputation in the earth. He stood in the gap between God's righteous judgments and the people's need for mercy. He boldly put his face into God's face.

The Consuming Fire

Thus the Lord GOD showed me, and behold, the Lord GOD was calling to contend with them by fire, and it consumed the great deep and began to consume the farm land. Then I said, "Lord GOD, please stop! How can Jacob stand, for he is small?" The LORD changed His mind about this. "This too shall not be," said the Lord GOD.

Amos 7:4-6

After his intervention regarding the locust judgment, Amos saw a second judgment coming. This time a consuming fire was about to be kindled against the farmland. Amos again cried, "Lord GOD, please stop! How can Jacob stand, for he is small?" (verse 5).

We need the same tenacious, watchful, responsive spirit in prayer. Normally when the Church wins a victory, we celebrate and maybe even relax our guard for a while. Amos did not do this. He remained keenly observant and prepared to intervene. The Lord changed His mind, therefore, about the judgment by fire: "This too shall not be" (verse 6).

"Lord GOD, Please Stop!"

Amos received five visions concerning the destiny of the nation. The first of these was the locust plague; the second was fire sweeping the nation. Both of these plagues were averted by the prayer of the prophet. Amos' third vision was of the plumb line revealing the nation's weak foundation. Fourth was the basket of summer fruits disclosing the nation's inner decay from repudiating God's Word. Herein it was proclaimed that a famine would come—not of bread and water, but of "hearing the words of the LORD" (Amos 8:11). The fifth and last vision revealed the hopelessness of escape from the vengeance of God (see 9:1-4).

These visions were progressive in nature. Each came with an opportunity for repentance. But each successive judgment seemed harder to avert.

159

We must repent, confess our unbelief toward an omnipotent God and cry to the Lord for the healing of the broken Body of His Son. Conquer the power of selfishness by choosing a life devoted to the cross. Repent of internal slander and bickering, and speak those things that give grace to the hearers. Cast off the spirit of fear and arise in the faith of our God. Break the bonds of religious ceremonialism and let the Spirit of liberty reign.

Modern Crisis Intercession

What I am about to tell you may blow your mind. It certainly did mine! But all these events are true, and I will tell you the story just as it happened.

In February 1994, I found myself in the Czech Republic for the Central European Reconciliation Conference. I was thrilled to be back in the beautiful homeland of rich church history of the likes of John Huss, the reformer excommunicated for revealing corruption in the clergy; and John Amos Comenius, bishop of the Bohemian Brethren who yearned for the unity of all Christians; and Count Zinzendorf, passionately devoted to Jesus, who longed to bring Christianity to the world.

The war in Sarajevo—the site of the beginning of World War I, where Archduke Francis Ferdinand was murdered—was at its height and threatening to escalate out of control. This was a volatile ethnic, regional and religious war. Catholics from Croatia, Orthodox from Serbia and Muslims from Bosnia Herzegovina were battling fiercely, committing horrible crimes against humanity in the process.

Before the prayer conference in Prague, I ministered for a few days to church leaders there. An American friend was my traveling intercessory companion.

One night my traveling assistant received a dream in which he saw three hunters with bows and arrows lined up ready to shoot. The last hunter hit the bull's-eye, and there was snow on the ground.

I knew the dream had something to do with the prayer conference we were about to attend, which I told my companion. However, we were very busy, and I thought little more about it.

A few days later we traveled north of Prague to participate in the reconciliation prayer conference. The purpose of the gathering: to bring delegates from across Europe to ask God to intervene in the horrific war in the former Yugoslavia. Pastoral and intercessory delegates assembled from countries as diverse as Hungary and Great Britain, Croatia and Belgium, Germany, Bulgaria and many other nations. (My friend and I were the only delegates from the Western Hemisphere.) The summit was chaired by Johannes Facius, international coordinator for the International Fellowship of Intercessors, and Dan Drapal, team leader of Christian Fellowship of Prague, Czech Republic.

A Pattern of Progressive Prayer

The prayer at that conference followed a pattern that had been discovered through trial and error over the years. It was unlike any prayer gathering I had ever attended—not because it was so intense, or even because it was tangibly anointed, but because of its patience.

The first day of prayer was spent in personal repentance. The main agenda was cleansing the land—this time, the land of our own hearts.

We spent the next day confessing the sins of the Church. We named the sins of our own congregations and denominations, both currently and historically. Often we had to turn to someone from a different background, humble ourselves and ask for forgiveness. At times it appeared little was happening, but patience prevailed.

On the third day we began to confess our national sins. The confessions of the first two days enabled us to delve more deeply into the sins of our ethnic groups and nations.

This is where it got all the more interesting. Tension rose as national and ethnic prejudices surfaced. But by the grace of God we continued to declare, "O Lord, please forgive us, for we have sinned." There were no great spiritual fireworks, just a pattern of progressive confession of sin.

By the fourth and final day, I had been in Europe for more than 25 days. I had not seen a newspaper that I could read, heard a radio program that I could understand or seen a television program that could clue me in to what was going on in the world. I was tired and took the afternoon to rest in my hotel room and seek the face of God.

A Strategic Encounter

Then it happened. In my room I began to hear airplanes circling overhead. They buzzed for some time. I couldn't figure it out. We were quite a distance from any airport, and they almost sounded like warplanes. What was happening?

Then I heard a word resound in the hotel room. It was not the still, quiet voice of God in my heart, but the external voice of the Lord speaking in the room: "If you do not pray, the planes will come." Then, in a vision of what looked like physical letters hanging against the wall, I read the name *Klaus*.

My spiritual antennas were out, and "knowing"—divine reasoning—came to me. Somehow—apart from any knowledge of current events—I knew that the guns of Serbia were poised in the mountains overlooking Sarajevo and ready to strike. Internally I knew that NATO was giving the Serbs 48 hours to remove their weapons from the mountains, or they would come and bomb out their sites. I also sensed that the Serbs were planning an attack of their own and that they, too, might send planes within 48 hours to bomb Sarajevo.

It was a crucial hour.

I waited and prayed some more, then left my room to look for the two primary leaders of the conference, Johannes Facius and Dan Drapal. In this setting I was a watchman, not an elder at the gate, and

I knew I was to submit the revelatory experience to the ones with delegated authority. Secretly I hoped that submitting the information to them might be all I had to do.

First I told Dan of the event.

"Do you know the names of our nation's governmental leaders?" he asked me.

I assured him I did not.

"The last name of the leader of the Czech government is Klaus," he said.

Interesting! Was this to signal the leaders that this experience was from God?

Then I found Johannes and shared the encounter with him. He, too, quizzed me, asking if I had been listening to the radio. Apparently they had just heard an emergency report a few minutes before, while I had been in my room, announcing that NATO had given the Serbs 48 hours to remove their artillery from the mountains surrounding Sarajevo or they would come with planes and bomb their entrenched sites. I was stunned.

The word God had spoken, however, was, "If you do not pray, the planes will come." And now we were headed into the last night's meeting.

The Three Hunters

After worship and teaching, Johannes called me to the front and asked me to share the word I had received. Unemotionally I told of the revelatory activity, then took my seat.

Then prayer time came. We had spent three days kneeling in personal repentance, humility and confession of sin. Now it was time to stand and fight. To my surprise, Johannes called three men—a prayer leader from England, another from Amsterdam and me—to lead us into aggressive intercession.

One after another, the three of us launched the prayers of intervention that the Lord gave us. I was the last in the lineup to fire away.

As I prayed, for a few seconds I was clothed with supernatural confidence and the authority of God. It might have been the gift of faith in operation in an intercessory dimension. In any case, it was as if I had been given a bow and arrow. It reminded me of my 1987 New York City prayer encounter about the Iranian action against the U.S. presence in Bahrain.

Feeling somewhat detached from my surroundings, I pulled back the string of the bow and released a powerful arrow of prayer for intervention.

"In the name of Jesus," I heard myself declaring, "I command the powers of darkness to back away from the mountains of Sarajevo, and that the planes will not come!"

Authority came upon me and then it lifted.

The meeting ended, and once again I was left with that familiar question, "Now what was *that* all about?" As I walked back to my seat, my assistant sounded excited.

"Do you remember the dream I told you about a few days ago?" he asked. "Remember how I saw three hunters and the third one hit the mark? Well, that just happened, and the third hunter was you!"

My American companion reminded me that at the end of the dream there had been snow on the ground. We both thought that was interesting. But the temperature now, even though it was February, was unseasonably warm.

That night, after the meeting had ended and we were all asleep, the temperature dropped dramatically—over 30 degrees Fahrenheit. The next morning we found a layer of beautiful white snow resting on the ground.

A sign from God? I believe so! We had confessed our sins—personal, ecclesiastical and national—and interceded on behalf of the war-torn region. Isaiah 1:18 gives us this insight:

> "Come now, and let us reason together," says the LORD, "though your sins are as scarlet, they will be as white as snow; though they are red like crimson, they will be like wool."

Maybe the Lord was giving us an indication in the natural realm, through the blanket of new snow, of genuine cleansing in the spiritual realm.

The Result

What actually transpired in 1994?

First, the Serbs pulled their guns out of the mountains. Second, no retaliatory warplanes were sent. And from that point, instead of escalating into a major war, this regional conflict began to wind down. God intervened through the power of intercession. Mercy triumphed over judgment once again.

The breakthrough was not the result of one prayer and reconciliation conference, of course. It was the result of God's people throughout the earth, lifting up a cry for crisis intervention, and then possibly—just possibly—God's authority being released into a specific setting.

Yes, take courage from this encounter to continue to fight for intervention in our day through humble, yet bold crisis intercession.

Applications for Us

You already know that I believe in crisis intervention through the power of prayer. Intercession draws a line in the sand and calls for darkness to end and for light to come. While judgment looms over the nations and perilous times are coming, let's not sit in the valley of despair.

Amos, like all the true prophets, did not leave his hearers in the depths of despair, but revealed the brightness of a new day. In the last word of his address, he declared God's promise to release His people from captivity and "plant them on their land, and they will not again be rooted out from their land which I have given them" (Amos 9:15).

In Amos' day judgment was partially averted or cut short. What will be the outcome in our day?

Get God's Perspective

In the midst of all this intense stuff, look up and get God's perspective. Remember, even judgment is ultimately for the purpose of redemption. Realize what Isaiah 26:9 says so well: "At night my soul longs for You, indeed, my spirit within me seeks You diligently; for when the earth experiences Your judgments the inhabitants of the world learn righteousness."

While I am one who emphasizes crying out to the Lord for intervention, there comes a time when God's judgments are His mercy. In that setting, just move aside and let God be God. He knows what is best and what is needed, and when. Yet keep on crying out all the while for mercy.

A Dose of Patience

In today's fast-food culture, the last thing we want to hear is "Wait!" or "Not yet!" And the last thing we want to do is follow a pattern of progressive praying, as the reconciliation conference followed step-by-step in Prague. Often we treat prayer as if we can drive up to a menu, place our order, pull forward to the service window and pick up our food—fresh and hot every time! At times the Lord whets our appetite with fast service. Often we find, however, that He is not only interested in giving us an answer but in making us into the solution. This recipe takes time and has that old-fashioned ingredient in it: patience.

Although there was a dramatic breakthrough at the prayer conference in Prague, what I took home with me was a fresh perspective on patience in the pattern of progressive praying.

A Life-Changing Encounter

In October 1998 I was honored to visit the Swansea Bible College that Rees Howells founded. I visited with his elderly son, Samuel Howells, who was 86 at the time and still an active intercessor. What a joy to be in the very room where his father led crisis intercession on behalf of the Jewish people in the days of World War II! A piece of history was sitting right before me in this divine interchange. I could feel the presence of holy angels as we talked about the past.

Doris M. Ruscoe, a student at Mr. Howells's Bible school, tells of some of these anointed prayer gatherings in her book *The Intercession of Rees Howells*.

> As each crisis in the war developed, the Holy Spirit guided our prayers and each time we knew that victory had been gained in the spirit before the news came over the radio or in the newspapers of victory on the field of battle. So great was the burden that there were times when Rees Howells could only wrestle alone with God in his room, while members of the staff carried on with the meetings.
>
> During the Battle of Britain, in the autumn of 1940, when Britain stood alone against the enemy and our airmen were fighting desperately to withstand the enemy attacks, especially on London, Rees Howells said, "Christian England will never be invaded." The enemy offensive, intended as a preliminary to invasion, came to a climax on September 15, a day we remember again for the assurance of victory. The attack failed and the invasion did not take place.[5]

We need this type of authority to be released once again. That is exactly why I went there on that visit to Wales—I was focused on my goal and would not turn back.

At the close of my appointment with Samuel Howells, I asked how his father had received such detailed revelation from God on what and how to pray. Did it come by dreams, visions, the burden of God—or just how? Mr. Howells would not answer me; he frankly avoided the subject. But I persisted. I asked two, three and, yes, even four times. "How did your father and those with him get this type of revelation and authority?"

With a tear trickling down his face, Mr. Howells's eventual remark to me was short and piercing: "Oh, you must understand, the Lord's servant was possessed by God."

That answered it all! New levels of authority with God and power over the enemy come from new levels of possession by God. I wept that afternoon as Mr. Howells laid his hands upon my shoulders and pronounced an impartation of his father's mantle.

What Is Required in This Hour?

The Holy Spirit is searching once again for a new generation of Daniels, Esthers, Deborahs and Josephs—for such a time as this. He is looking for you. It is time for the grace of crisis intercession to be poured out once again. As the Lord's jealousy draws near, yield!

In fact, I believe His presence is available right now. I have a word for you in closing—"Be possessed by God!" Yes, you can be possessed by the Holy Spirit of God.

This indeed is the key to all effectiveness in life and ministry. This was the key of Jesus, our glorious Messiah, and all the pilgrims of the faith who have followed in His footsteps. And this indeed is the key to crisis intercession.

Be possessed by God!

Practical Applications—Making It Real!

- Ask the Lord to prepare your heart for crisis intervention through intercession. Seek the Lord for revelation for this kind of authority in prayer.
- Pick a tragedy in the earth today and begin to lift up a cry for mercy for those severely affected.
- Take the Scripture promise of Jeremiah 29:11 and meditate on it. Now remind the Lord of His Word on this current situation by praying the promise back to Him.
- Ask the Lord for a spirit of faith to rebuke the enemy in Jesus' name concerning this crisis situation.

Recommended Reading

Rees Howells: Intercessor by Norman Grubb (Lutterworth Press, 2003)

Shaping History through Prayer and Fasting: How Christians Can Change World Events through the Simple Yet Powerful Tools of Prayer and Fasting by Derek Prince (Revell, 1973)

The Intercession of Rees Howells by Doris M. Ruscoe (Zerubbabel Press, 2003)

Authority in Prayer: Praying with Power and Purpose by Dutch Sheets (Bethany House, 2006)

11

Wisdom Issues

AT VARIOUS TIMES in my life I have asked for the power of God to set the captives free. (I still do.) I have cried out for finances to be able to extend His Kingdom. (I still need this, too.) On other occasions I have pleaded for the holiness of God. (I am still desperate for this.) Many times I have sought the Lord for a compassionate and merciful heart. (I really continue after this one as well.)

There seems to be no end to the list of things we need from God. Yet, we must learn to pray for the long haul, rather than just flare up like a Roman candle display. Intense prayers shooting up into the night with a brilliant flash may prompt "oohing" and "aahing," only to fizzle out as quickly as they shot up. If I were given only one thing to ask for, I would follow the example of King Solomon and request wisdom for life's journey. It is the ingredient necessary for the long haul.

One of the three Holy Spirit-inspired prayers from my youth—"Give me wisdom beyond my years"—is a prayer I will continue to lift up. I need wisdom more today than yesterday, and I will surely need more tomorrow than I do today.

Intimacy for War

Although I have never served in active military duty, I have fought in many "air" wars. I have spent sleepless nights watching and waiting for orders from my Commander-in-Chief, on the alert for whatever was needed next. I have spent days fasting, not just because of Jesus' loveliness but out of desperation for help or because my heart was breaking for someone.

This part of the Christian life is not just about wine and roses, intimate times and hangin' with Jesus. I actually prefer the romance of being the Bride of Christ. But that is not all there is. We need to be the fighting Bride (see Ephesians 5:25–27; 6:13–18). We must hold tightly to God's hand (intimacy) while moving out with His authority (warfare). It is not one or the other; it is intimacy in order to war effectively. As the title of one of Francis Frangipane's books aptly declares, "This day we fight!"

But it takes guts to be in the army. We need courage in today's society. Why? Because serving in the military is tough. When you hit the enemy, he likes to hit back. One of the tricks for surviving the battle is to be like a rhinoceros with a thick skin and a big heart. I don't have that one down yet. Many of us, in fact, tend to be either hard-hearted or thin-skinned. But somehow, as we grow in wisdom, we must learn to be both tough and tender.

Wisdom Lessons from the Trenches

But where do we as intercessors and soldiers begin in our quest for wisdom? We may love and desire wisdom, but how do we actually obtain it? Far too often we ask God for wisdom only to get in way over our heads. We find the highways of spiritual warfare littered with casualties. We push along, ignoring warning signals that a curve lies ahead, and end up in a ditch or stalled along the roadside, burned out for Jesus simply through overheating or sheer exhaustion.

I have been around this mountain a few times myself, and have seen many people running like hamsters on a wheel of misfortune. Let me share some lessons I am learning in the trenches regarding the pitfalls and perils of intercessory warfare. God will give us wisdom if we ask Him (see James 1:5), but like good soldiers in training, we have to learn how to use it.

Let's proceed, then, with ten distinct wisdom applications for intercessors.

1. Get a Life!

Often it seems that people involved in prophetic, intercessory and spiritual warfare are so engaged in the seriousness of their task that they miss the joy of common, everyday living. Some of us try so hard to discern every breeze, or to interpret the significance of every bird that flies by the window that we become granola Christians—nutty, flaky and fruity!

My basic counsel is, get a life. Go for a walk; it will help your soul. Find a hobby; it will do you good. Go work out at the health club. Exercise and release the tension. Your physical body will thank you and others might like you better. And who knows? You might even make a new friend. Do not forget to take care of yourself—rest, exercise, eat well—and don't neglect friendships and fun. As one of my friends has said, "Learn to laugh at life, yourself and the enemy. Kick up your heels and enjoy the ride!"

Do not just watch life; live it! For Jesus' sake, yours and your family's, get a life.

Wow, point number one was really heavy, wasn't it?

2. Avoid Criticizing at All Costs

Do you know what undoes intercessory groups more than anything else? It is not lack of vision, leadership or even an overt counterattack. It is the immature application of discernment expressed through criticism. This can lead to backstabbing, which left unaddressed will cause the group to splinter and the devil to win again. How? Through subtle, simple, old-fashioned criticism. It is impossible to pray together with criticism in your midst.

Once I attended an "Intercessors for America" conference in Washington, D.C. At one of the sessions the jealousy of the Holy Spirit came on me and I began to prophesy. I remember the word clearly:

> We are now living in the time of the coexistence of the house of David and the house of Saul. You who have been waiting, yearning, believing, longing and praying for the house of David to come forth can disqualify yourselves from being part of what you've been waiting, yearning, praying and believing for, if you sow accusation and critical speech toward the house of Saul while it yet stands. For remember, you, too, have come forth from Saul's loins.

Discernment must be stewarded carefully. We will either turn it into private intercession or gossip and slander. Criticism does not just affect the person hearing the word; when passed around, it holds back the whole community.

Avoid criticism at all costs.

3. Forgiveness Is a Necessity

Second Corinthians 2:10–11 brings us a great wisdom application for all areas of the Christian life—all the more important for intercessors and leaders:

> Whom you forgive anything, I forgive also; for indeed what I have forgiven, if I have forgiven anything, I did it for your sakes in the presence of Christ, so that no advantage would be taken of us by Satan, for we are not ignorant of his schemes.

Peter wrote: "God is opposed to the proud, but gives grace to the humble" (1 Peter 5:5). When you confess your sins to another, you become a candidate to receive grace. Confession is an act of humility. The proud never confess they are wrong. They cannot see their own faults. But the humble confess their sins and thus receive grace. Healing begins to flow in and through vessels of grace. This is why James 5:16 says to "confess your sins to one another, and pray for one another so that you may be healed."

Forgiveness is not an option; it is a necessity. I, for one, believe it is one of the most powerful weapons of spiritual warfare. The apostle Paul was saying in 2 Corinthians 2:10–11 that when we forgive, we take the advantage away from Satan. Like Paul, then, let's not be ignorant of Satan's schemes. Forgive and turn the tables on the devil. Shut the door on him and extend grace to others by walking in forgiveness.

4. Stick with Your Highest Weapons

At one point I went to Atlanta to pray with my friends Gene and Pat Gastineau and their prayer ministry. While I was there, Pat and I were discussing spiritual warfare tactics and she gave me some wise counsel.

"The Lord has given you and Michal Ann an anointing in worship and praise warfare," she said. "Don't try to put on *our* shoes. Wear what God has given you. You need to stay with your highest weapons."

Now that was wisdom! It was as though I could hear my Master's voice in those words.

As it is in natural war, so it is in spiritual warfare. Before you send in the ground troops, you send in the air patrol. Let's be wise! Bomb out the enemy's bunkers first through the weapons of high praise. Stay with it long enough to get the Holy Spirit's witness—peace, knowing, certainty—then send in the ground troops, shooting the artillery at specifically determined targets.

I would like to add a few words about praise, since that is one of the highest weapons. Praise, like prayer, is a weapon we all can wield. Remember, God uses our praise to bind up the enemy. Psalm 149:5–9 powerfully depicts this:

Let the godly ones exult in glory; let them sing for joy on their beds. Let the high praises of God be in their mouth, and a two-edged sword in their hand, to execute vengeance on the nations and punishment on the peoples, to bind their kings with chains and their nobles with fetters of iron, to execute on them the judgment written; this is an honor for all His godly ones. Praise the LORD!

It "is an honor for all His godly ones" (verse 9). Well, beloved, guess who "all" includes? We all get to tie up the enemy's works by declaring what the Word of God, the two-edged sword, says and by lavishly praising the Lord.

Yes, praise is effective. Know *your* highest weapon and use it mightily.

5. *Stick Close to the Blood*

There is a principle that runs throughout the Scriptures: "The life of the flesh is in the blood" (Leviticus 17:11). Not only is there life in the blood, but innocent blood, when shed, has a particular attribute: It cries out. The blood of Abel spilled on the ground could be heard by the Lord. He came running to find out what was going on. Perhaps Abel's blood was releasing a screech: "Vengeance! I want vengeance!"

Before the presence of our Judge in heaven, there is blood that speaks louder than the blood of Abel. What does this blood declare? The blood of Jesus reminds the Father continuously of the sacrifice of His sinless Son. The blood of Jesus ever cries out, "Mercy! Mercy! Mercy!"

Scripture recounts many benefits concerning what the blood of Jesus has done for us. According to Revelation 12:11 the believers "overcame [the accuser of the brethren] because of the blood of the Lamb and because of the word of their testimony, and they did not love their life even when faced with death." Let's look at a few of these biblical benefits:

1. We have been forgiven (see Hebrews 9:22–28).
2. We have been cleansed from all sin (see 1 John 1:7).

3. We have been redeemed (see Ephesians 1:7).

4. We have been justified—"just-as-if-I'd" never sinned (see Romans 5:9).

5. We have been set apart (sanctified) for a holy calling (see Hebrews 13:12).

6. We have found peace (see Colossians 1:20).

7. We have confidence to enter the holy place (see Hebrews 10:19).

Do you know the safest place to be? Close to the blood. We overcome by testifying to what the blood of Jesus has accomplished. Yes, stick close to and testify to what the blood of Jesus Christ has accomplished.

6. *The Necessity of Compassion*

What is compassion? It is the quality needed to move in the works of Christ. *Webster's* says it is the sympathetic consciousness of another's distress together with a desire to alleviate it. Ken Blue, in his book *The Authority to Heal*, states:

> The kind of compassion Jesus was said to have for people was not merely an expression of His will but rather an eruption from deep within His being. Out of this compassion of Jesus sprang forth His mighty works of rescue, healing, and deliverance.[1]

Everything Jesus did and does relates to who He is. Everything we do is connected with who Jesus is in and through us. In order to be effective—whether for street-level evangelism, apostolic missions or any other ministry—we must have a current revelation of God's nature in and toward us. We must know the Father's love to move in His love. Otherwise we engage in nothing more than a bunch of obligatory religious works.

Consider the following verses, given in various translations, to fuel your fire of compassion.

[God], being full of compassion, forgave their iniquity, and did not destroy them. Yes, many a time He turned His anger away, and did not stir up all His wrath; for He remembered that they were but flesh, a breath that passes away and does not come again.

Psalm 78:38–39, NKJV

You, O Lord, are a compassionate and gracious God, slow to anger, abounding in love and faithfulness.

Psalm 86:15, NIV

This I recall and therefore have I hope and expectation: It is because of the Lord's mercy and loving-kindness that we are not consumed, because His [tender] compassions fail not. They are new every morning; great and abundant is Your stability and faithfulness.

Lamentations 3:21–23, AMPLIFIED

Do you get the picture? Our Father's nature is one of love, patience, loving-kindness and mercy. Learn compassion. Declare as my wife, Michal Ann, does, "Compassion acts!" Yes, gird yourself with compassion, realizing it is an amazing force that ultimately propels you to action.

7. No Common Ground with Evil

In John 14:30, an eye-opening verse, Jesus is talking about His authority over the devil: "I will not speak much more with you, for the ruler of the world is coming, and he has nothing in Me." The Amplified Bible gives us some insight into this passage in the way it translates this last phrase: "He has no claim on Me. [He has nothing in common with Me; there is nothing in Me that belongs to him, and he has no power over Me.]"

Do you see the correlation? Terry Crist, in his book *Interceding against the Powers of Darkness*, casts light for us on this subject:

The reason Jesus was so effective in spiritual warfare . . . why He was able to confront the devil so effectively . . . in the wilderness encounter [was that] Jesus recognized the law of purification. The reason Jesus could stand in such power and authority and deal so effectively with the wicked oppressor of the nations was because no common ground existed between Him and His adversary. When the devil struck at Jesus, there was nothing whatsoever in Him to receive the "hit." When Satan examined Him, there was nothing for him to find. Jesus and Satan had no relationship one to another, no common ground. There was nothing in Jesus that bore witness with the works of darkness! One reason so many ministers and intercessors have been spiritually "hit" by the fiery darts of the enemy is because they have not responded to the law of purification.[2]

Let me try to explain this vital matter.

Before you go chasing after external dragons and territorial spirits, make sure there is nothing you hold in common with the enemy. Let the finger of God probe into your heart, mind and actions. Open up to conviction concerning your life, family, church or ministry. Repent when necessary. Bring cleansing to your own life through the power of the blood of Jesus and yield to the work of the cross. Destroy the legal basis—the right of the enemy—to attack you. Then you can take authority over the external enemies without receiving the horrendous repercussions of inept spiritual warfare.

Sometimes sincere, gifted believers have common ground with the enemy and prematurely wage war against the very power of darkness that has a foothold in their own lives. Let the finger of God inside you to conquer your personal enemies. Then you will have assurance to defeat the spirits of wickedness in the heavenly places!

8. Avoid Lures

Have you ever gone fishing? A smart fish does not bite at everything that floats by. Personally I love to fish for trout. They have keen eyesight and do not go after every lure. Trout have to be convinced that the bait is right before they make a commitment.

Perhaps we should "go to the trout" to learn a lesson. Do not chase after every lure that comes along. Lures can be distractions. When the devil shows his head, keep your focus on Jesus. At times the enemy intentionally manifests his presence just to derail our pure devotion to Jesus. He is trying to capture and keep our attention.

Remember, when the devil knocks, send Jesus to answer! That might sound trite, but I don't mean it like that. One of the ways we can do this is by simply not giving the devil the time of day. Do not follow him! We are called to follow Jesus. We must "[fix] our eyes on Jesus, the author and perfecter of faith" (Hebrews 12:2).

This is simple but powerful. As we maintain our focus on the Lord, He releases His presence and overpowers the enemy. I am not diminishing the power of confrontational, authoritative prayer or rebuking the enemy in the name of Jesus. I fully embrace the extraordinary teaching of Dutch Sheets in his book *Authority in Prayer*. It is an arrow in my quiver! I am merely reminding you to choose the fights and battles you enter into. Avoid being seduced by lures. Keep your gaze fixed on Jesus, and let Him guide your use of authority.

9. Break the Penalty

By *break the penalty* I mean "neutralize the backlash of spiritual warfare."

I pulled this gem from the life of Gideon:

Gideon took ten men of his servants and did as the LORD had spoken to him; and because he was too afraid of his father's household and the men of the city to do it by day, he did it by night. When the men of the city arose early in the morning, behold, the altar of Baal was torn down, and the Asherah which was beside it was cut down, and the second bull was offered on the altar which had been built. They said to one another, "Who did this thing?" And when they searched about and inquired, they said, "Gideon the son of Joash did this thing." Then the men of the city said to Joash, "Bring out your son, that he may die, for he has torn down the altar of Baal, and indeed, he has cut down the Asherah which was beside it." But Joash said to all who stood against him, "Will you contend for Baal, or will you deliver him? Whoever will plead for him shall be put to death by morning. If he is a god, let him contend for himself, because some-one has torn down his altar." Therefore on that day he named him Jerubbaal, that is to say, "Let Baal contend against him," because he had torn down his altar.

Judges 6:27–32

Here we find that a penalty—a curse or consequence—was put into place to fall on the one who would tear down the demonic high places. The Scripture does not explicitly say this, but we may infer it by the command the men of the city gave to Gideon's father: "Bring out your son, that he may die" (verse 30). Gideon's father, who owned the altar to Baal, had probably released a demonic stronghold or force to war against whoever would tear down the altar of false worship to Baal. Now he renamed his son Jerubbaal, "Let Baal contend against him" (verse 32).

Some spiritual warfare specialists inform us that professional witchcraft practitioners pronounce curses (or penalties) particularly on those who threaten their kingdom. The Old Testament picture from the life of Gideon gives us insight into the necessity of praying a hedge of protection around ourselves and our families, and break-ing, in the name of Jesus, any curse or penalty that the enemy tries to enforce on God's people when they are confronting darkness.

Notice also God's reward for his valiant warriors: "The Spirit of the LORD came upon Gideon" (Judges 6:34). Literally this means that God's Spirit *clothed* Gideon. He actually took possession of him. So take heart. The reward from God can be awesome!

After engaging in a power encounter with the enemy, I have learned from experience to offer up a prayer breaking any possible counterattack that the enemy would release against me. This includes attacks against my family members, health, hope, future, calling, finances, possessions, vehicles, pets, etc. The prayer goes like this: *In the name of Jesus, and by the power of His blood shed on the cross, I command the penalty of the enemy, any word curse that has been pronounced against me and any backlash of the evil one sent against me and my family, to be broken. It shall not prosper as I nullify its effect in Jesus' mighty name. I proclaim a blessing to all that I am, hope to be and put my hand to, and to all that pertains to my life, health, home, finances, ministry and family. I call forth strength, vigor, protection and the supply of the Lord, for the honor and glory of His name. Amen.*

Hey, it makes sense. Have *you* blocked the counterattack from coming?

10. The Safety Net: Walking with Others

This is an important part of wisdom. Ecclesiastes 4:9–12 aptly remarks:

> Two are better than one because they have a good return for their labor. For if either of them falls, the one will lift up his companion. But woe to the one who falls when there is not another to lift him up. Furthermore, if two lie down together they keep warm, but how can one be warm alone? And if one can overpower him who is alone, two can resist him. A cord of three strands is not quickly torn apart.

Look at this more closely. We all fall down occasionally for one reason or another. Isn't it wonderful that the Lord provides others to help us up when we get knocked down?

Check out another aspect of this safety net, too: "Two can resist him" (verse 12). This is an awesome promise to remember, to claim, to proclaim and to kneel on. "Five of you shall chase a hundred, and a hundred of you shall put ten thousand to flight; your enemies shall fall by the sword before you" (Leviticus 26:8, NKJV). Our power over the devil multiplies when we join with others.

Do you have a partner in prayer with whom you walk? Who is watching your back? The armor of God protects our front side, but we become one another's rear guard. Let's cover one another with godly counsel, fellowship and prayer.

"Every Finney needs a Father Nash," writes Dick Eastman, "and every preacher needs an intercessor."[3] I believe this, and have given myself to other ministries over the years to be an Aaron or Hur to help hold up their hands through the power of prevailing prayer. And I am grateful today that there are those who stand with Encounters Network in our many endeavors.

You can be used of the Lord to help raise up "the shield of faith" (Ephesians 6:16) on behalf of others. May every ministry have its prayer shield raised up in Jesus' name!

Engaging in the Battle

Before we turn the final corner to the subject of gatekeepers opening the way for God's presence, let me highlight one more thought on the subject of wisdom issues for intercessors: Not every battle is yours. Some are for you; some are for others. Some battles are for today; some are for another day. Some are simply not yours to engage in at all.

Cry out to the Lord with me for discernment and wisdom beyond all our years. Maybe you should even join me, like a child, kneeling in humble adoration.

Lord, give me wisdom beyond my years. Father, grant to me the spirit of wisdom and revelation in the knowledge of the glorious Lord Jesus Christ. May I be preserved by Your hand to become a veteran for the people of the next generation, to pass on to them treasures from the war chest. In Jesus' name. Amen.

Practical Applications—Making It Real!

- Pray through the book of Proverbs, asking the Father to give you wisdom beyond your years.

- Ask the Lord to reveal areas of wisdom in which you are weak and to teach you to incorporate them into your life.
- Gain further wisdom by asking questions of those wiser than you. Interview an older believer in Christ.
- Ask the Lord to root out areas of unforgiveness and criticism so you can be a greater channel of blessing to others.
- Ask the Holy Spirit to put His finger of conviction on your heart. Confess and repent in order to close any doorways of your life and family to the enemy. Then pray the prayers, in Jesus' name, canceling the penalty against your life, family and ministry.

Recommended Reading

The Spiritual Fight by Pat Gastineau (Word of Love, 1997)

Passion for Jesus: Perfecting Extravagant Love for God by Mike Bickle (Charisma House, 1993)

The Way of the Warrior: How to Fulfill Life's Most Difficult Assignments by Harry Jackson Jr. (Chosen, 2005)

12

Breakers and Gatekeepers

THE "BREAKERS" ARE coming! These are the prophetic intercessors that help give birth to the purposes of God for their generation, and they are appearing once again. We need breakthrough in today's society, but there is no breakthrough without a breaker.

Micah 2:13 describes the activity we will examine in this chapter: "The breaker goes up before them; they break out, pass through the gate and go out by it. So their king goes on before them, and the LORD at their head."

Truly the Lord Jesus Himself is our breaker—the One who has gone before us and broken open the gates of heaven and hell. He has done it all. But today, as in the days of John the Baptist and other strategic breakers, the Holy Spirit is looking for those who will go ahead of the pack, blaze a trail in the spirit and open the way, that the Lord may "pass through the gate" among them.

Let the breakers arise! Let the breaker anointing be released! Let breakthrough come!

Open Heavens in the Word of God

As I have studied revival, I have found a peculiar term that relates to the concept of breakthrough: *open heavens*. In recent days and months I have found myself pondering this amazing subject. Once again I went on a search with my Bible. Let's take a quick peek at some of these verses.

Ezekiel 1:1 states that "the heavens were opened and I saw visions of God." As the heavens open, Ezekiel describes a great cloud, sent by God to protect him from His brightness. Can you imagine such a sight? Then Ezekiel sees "fire flashing forth continually" (verse 4) or lightning, bright light, angels and other glorious details.

Several other Old Testament passages describe similar experiences in which the heavens parted and the heavenly came down to earth or man was somehow caught up into the heavenlies. Consider the transforming visionary experience of Isaiah: he was shown the glory of God, the fire of purification and the message of "Whom shall I send, and who will go for Us?" (Isaiah 6:8). Likewise Daniel, as he received visions in the night, saw the Lord "like a Son of Man" coming through "the clouds of heaven" taking up His throne before the Ancient of Days (Daniel 7:13). Awesome!

Fast forward to the New Testament. At Jesus' very own baptism, as recorded in Matthew 3:16–17, "the heavens were opened" and the Holy Spirit descends on the Son of God in the form of a dove. Then the Father speaks audibly: "This is My beloved Son, in whom I am well-pleased" (verse 17).

In Acts we find Stephen, the flaming deacon, being stoned to death for preaching the Gospel. As he is dying, he sees "the heavens opened up and the Son of Man standing at the right hand of God" (Acts 7:56). The sky is loosened, the clouds are rolled back and Jesus is standing to receive him. What a sight! What a cost! But what a privilege!

John, the disciple who lays his head on Jesus' heart, has a profound experience recorded in the book of Revelation. John, now imprisoned and eighty years old, is "in the Spirit on the Lord's day" (Revelation

1:10). As he meditates on his Beloved, he sees "a door standing open in heaven" (Revelation 4:1) and hears a voice calling him. He is not only able to peer into the heavenly realm, but he is told to "come up here" (verse 1). As he does, he sees the One who sits on the throne, as the elders, angels and four living creatures all worship radically in the beauty of holiness. As a result John receives many detailed messages from the glorified Lord Jesus Christ.

Openings as Gateways in the Spirit

What are open heavens and how do they occur? Are there any today? The Holy Spirit is turning His spotlight on this subject in the days ahead. Let me give you a possible definition of this phenomenon from my book *The Seer* that resulted from my research.

> An "open heaven" is a vision where a hole seems to appear in the immediate sky, the celestial realm is disclosed and heavenly sights of God become seeable. The term "open heaven" originated in historic revivals to describe those times when the manifested presence of God seems to come down in a tangible manner as conviction of sin, conversions, and healings take place. We are now moving from an ear of prophetic renewal into a new epoch of the Holy Spirit. We are crossing a threshold into a period of apostolic open heavens for whole cities and regions to be visited by the presence of the Almighty.[1]

Some call these portals "thresholds" or "gateways" in the spiritual realm. I believe there are entry points, spiritual hot spots, where God's presence becomes tangible. Remember the lesson concerning those who waited at the pool of Bethesda? At certain seasons an angel of the Lord was released and stirred the water, and the first person to step into the anointed waters was healed (see John 5:1–4). It is my conviction that there are gateways where God's presence seems to invade earthly space and time in a powerful way.

In the natural, gates are used to keep certain things out and let other things in. The elders are to sit at the gates of the city (see Proverbs 31:23) and permit or deny entrance into their regions. So it is in the spiritual realm. Isaiah 60:18 tells us, "You will call your walls salvation, and your gates praise." We need walls of protection around every believer, family and church. Psalm 100:4 tells us that we "enter His gates with thanksgiving and His courts with praise."

Not only are we called to enter the presence of the King with thanksgiving through the gates of praise, but we are likewise to overtake the gateways of the enemy. Jesus said, "Upon this rock I will build My church; and the gates of Hades will not overpower it" (Matthew 16:18).

A marvelous book by Cindy Jacobs of Generals of Intercession, *Possessing the Gates of the Enemy*, teaches more about this, based on the verse, "Your seed shall possess the gate of their enemies," found in Genesis 22:17.

The Holy Spirit is now reopening prophetic gateways between heaven and earth. The enemy has come along, as he did in the time of Abraham and Isaac, and filled up the wells of salvation. Now the time has come for breakers to redig these ancient wells and allow the waters of God's healing presence to flow once again (see Genesis 26:15–22). I believe we will then move past redigging old wells and open up entire new regions for Jesus Christ. This is a part of the coming prophetic revolution.

A Historic Example

A revival took place in 1949 in the village of Barvas on the largest island of the Outer Hebrides off the northwest coast of Scotland. Much has been written about the impact of pastor/evangelist Duncan Campbell and the meetings he led in that time. But little attention has been paid to the prayer warriors who paved the way before and during that mighty move of God's presence.

Behind the scenes labored two elderly sisters: Peggy Smith, who was 84 years old and blind; and her sister, Christine Smith, 82 years old and almost doubled over with arthritis. They were unable to attend regular church services, but for months they prayed in their home for God to send revival to Barvas. These two relentless intercessors prayed by name for the people in each cottage along their village streets. They reminded God of His Word in Isaiah 44:3: "I will pour water upon him that is thirsty, and floods upon the dry ground" (KJV). They cried this prophetic promise to the Lord day and night.

Across the village, independent of the Smith sisters, seven young men met three nights a week in a barn to pray for revival. They made a covenant with God and one another, according to Isaiah 62:6–7, that they would give Him no rest until He sent revival their way. Month after month they prevailed in prayer.

One night in particular they prayed with fervency Psalm 24:3–5: "Who shall ascend into the hill of the LORD? or who shall stand in his holy place? He that hath clean hands, and a pure heart. . . . He shall receive the blessing . . . from the God of his salvation" (KJV). Instantly, it seemed, the barn was filled with the glory of God and the young men praying from the Psalms fell prostrate on the floor. An awesome awareness of God overcame them and they were drenched with supernatural power they had never known before.

At that very time, the Lord gave one of the Smith sisters a vision. Peggy Smith saw the churches crowded with people, and hundreds being swept into the Kingdom of God. They sent word to their pastor that they had "broken through" and that heaven was about to descend on earth.

And so it did. The whole region seemed saturated with God. Wherever people were—in the workplace, in their homes or on the roads—they were overwhelmed by the presence of almighty God. Water indeed soaked the dry ground as Holy Spirit conviction was poured out in those days. A stream of blessing flowed that brought hundreds to salvation during the days of that historic visitation.[2]

189

Now let me be vulnerable with you and share one of the most dramatic prophetic encounters from my own life that illustrates a gateway of the Spirit.

Encounter at the Lake

It was a quiet Wednesday evening in May 1989. Michal Ann and I had just returned home from a meeting in nearby Kansas City. I was restless and we both knew it. I had to be alone with the Lord; something was up. So Michal Ann blessed me, and I got into our car and went on a drive. It was about 9 P.M.

I could hear the still, small voice of the dove of God speaking in my heart. He would say, *Turn here. Turn right. Go there.* His presence was very near. Eventually I drove up to a man-made, recreational body of water called Longview Lake, not far from our home in South Kansas City. Even the names of the roads leading there seemed prophetic: Longview Road and Highland Drive. And later that night I did experience a long look at a higher place into which Jesus wants to bring His Body.

As I drove, I came to a part of the lake that I had never seen before. I parked my car and stepped outside. Immediately to my left I saw a road that looked familiar. I had seen that gravel road earlier that day in a vision. So I proceeded to walk down the narrow road, which led to an arm of land jutting out into the lake. There, at the end of this path, was a concrete block building with a high wire fence around it. It seemed to be some kind of a powerhouse or generator.

Then something—or maybe I should say Someone, that wonderful Guide and Revealer of truth, the Holy Spirit—seemed to take over. I heard His gentle voice within me say, *Walk around the powerhouse seven times, praying in the Spirit.*

So I obeyed.

No one was out on the lake that night—no boats, no fishermen. It was a beautiful, serene, still night, even though it had rained recently.

I walked around once, praying very quietly with the gift of tongues. I walked around a second and third time. As I continued on my journey of obedience, I found myself praying more loudly with each round. By the time I was walking around for the seventh time, I was praying loudly in the language the Holy Spirit gave me.

When I had completed my seventh trip, I heard His voice again: *Walk around the powerhouse an eighth time, declaring into the heavens.*

Without even pondering what He meant, I headed off. I walked up to the first corner of the fence surrounding the building, stopped, peered into heaven and raised my right arm toward the sky. Out of my mouth came a powerful, spontaneous declaration: "Open be the way! Open be the way! Open be the way for the beginning of a great visitation."

After releasing this proclamation, I headed off to the next corner, stopped, raised my arm, stared into the sky and again declared, "Open be the way! Open be the way! Open be the way for the beginning of a great visitation."

I proceeded to the third and the fourth corners, doing the same.

When I had completed my fourth proclamation, I thought perhaps that was all I was to do that night, and I started to turn and walk away. But the voice of the dove came into my heart again: *I want you to go down to the bank of the muddy lake below and strike the waters.*

Well, my human reasoning was turned off and His divine reasoning was turned on. So I mused, *If I'm going to strike the waters, then surely, on whatever path I choose, there will be a branch along the way that I will pick up to strike the waters with.*

Off I went, sauntering through the weeds. Sure enough, along the path I saw a large branch from a tree. I picked it up and Jeremiah 23:5–6 lit up inside me. *There is One who is called the righteous Branch,* I thought as I continued making my way down to the muddy bank of the lake below.

When I arrived there I saw a wood plank resting on the muddy bank of this man-made lake. I stepped onto it.

While I stood there, the branch in my hand, the Holy Spirit said, *Another fisherman has stood here before you.* (Hold that thought; I will return to it later.)

Then, as I stood on the wood plank with the branch raised high in the air, I heard these words: *Strike the waters.*

I lowered the branch onto the still water directly in front of me. Then something strange began to take place. Dark, shadowy lines began to form in the middle of the lake, coming toward me. These lines began to take on the shape of waves. I continued to watch as the water swept over my feet on the shore. The atmosphere around me was charged with fear.

"Lord, I'm afraid!" I cried aloud.

At that very moment the waves ceased. Instantly the lake became once again like a sheet of glass. I was startled, amazed and frightened all at the same time.

The persistent Lamb spoke into my being again: *Release a song of love to the Holy Spirit in order to woo the return of His presence.*

I stood on that wood plank and sang out a song of love to the Holy Spirit, inviting His presence to return.

Then I heard it again: *Strike the waters.*

As I lowered the branch the second time onto the water, immediately in front of me, dark, shadowy lines again appeared in the middle of the lake and rippled toward me. They grew in intensity, power and thrust. Waves of water began to pound onto the shore and around my feet. This time, however, the atmosphere around me was charged with joy, faith and excitement. I stood there, praising the Lord aloud, celebrating and enjoying His presence.

When the waves subsided and the manifest presence of God abated, I decided to start back up the gravel road and head home.

Then He spoke to me for the last time that night: *All I have ever required of My people is two things: that they believe Me and that they do whatever little thing I have commanded them to do.*

Then He personalized it, imprinting His message onto my consciousness: *And all I am requiring of you is two things: that you believe Me for the beginning of this great visitation and that you obey whatever little thing I command you to do.*

I walked on up the road, got into my car and drove home. It was late now, and when I arrived home, Michal Ann was already asleep. As I got into bed, the anointing of God's manifest presence began to wear off.

Now what was that? I wondered.

Throwing up one of those feeble "Help me, God!" kinds of prayers, I dozed off.

Interpreting the Encounter

The next day, Thursday, I told Michal Ann about the event. I do not recall relaying it to anyone else. That Saturday morning I received a phone call from an older Christian gentleman who is a seasoned, prophetic seer named Bob Jones. I will never forget the conversation.

"I saw you in a vision this morning," he remarked. "You and I were walking down a gravel road together. It led to some kind of powerhouse. Then waves of water began coming up on our feet. Does that mean anything to you?"

I sighed and responded quickly, "Yes, it means two things to me. One, I am not crazy, and, two, it confirms the meaning of a profound divine encounter I have just experienced."

I proceeded to explain to Bob what had transpired three days earlier and thanked him for his confirming word. Good old Bob just listened to me. He knew almost all the details, it seemed, before I got them out of my mouth!

What did this unusual encounter mean? First, the Lord calls forth prophetic intercessors that are "captured," as Elijah was in 1 Kings 18, by a sound in the Spirit that has not yet been heard in the natural. Yes, the answers, as in Elijah's day, seem to come first like a cloud the size of a man's hand. But we must never "[despise] the day of small things" (Zechariah 4:10).

With a word burning within, these breakers look up into the heavens and, like God, call "things that are not as though they were" (Romans 4:17, NIV). They are captivated by a vision of what is yet to come. Seeing clouds heavy with rain, they take a knife of the Spirit and split the heavens open, calling forth the promised rainfall of His presence.

Thus the cry comes: "Open be the way! Open be the way!" This cry is not directed to crowds of men and women but to the balconies of heaven. We must proclaim God's will and Word, pierce the darkness of the hindering powers of the enemy and call out that the gates of heaven be opened up once again.

Remember how I stumbled onto the branch? It represents the work of the cross that each of us is called to carry. The Holy Spirit is seeking those who will lift up the completed work of the cross. When this righteous Branch is lifted up, Jesus draws all men to Himself (see John 12:32).

Yes, let's lift up Jesus. The primacy of our message is not that of movements and streams and denominations. In fact, our message is not even the preaching of the Church. It is Christ Jesus crucified and risen from the dead (see 1 Corinthians 2:2; 2 Corinthians 4:5; Galatians 6:14). There is no deeper message than the simple, "foolish" preaching of the cross (see 1 Corinthians 1:18–25). Let's extravagantly lift up Jesus!

The Two Waves

Just as I lowered the branch two times onto the water at Longview Lake, followed by two releases of waves, so I am convinced that there are two great waves of God's manifest presence and glory coming to the Church in this generation.

First is a wave of His presence, restoring the fear of the Lord. This has been a missing ingredient in a generation that has sought the hand of God (His blessing) at times, but not the face of God Himself.

This magnificent first wave of grace will be followed, I believe, by an extraordinary surge upon surge of power evangelism flowing across the nations. As the fear of the Lord is restored to the Bride of Christ, the power of God will flow as rarely seen since the days of the book of Acts. We are on the verge of a tidal wave of His presence.

The combination of these two great movements will usher in a great end-time harvest for the Lord's glory. O Lord, let it come!

A Few Simple Words

The first time I described my experience at Longview Lake publicly (I told you I would come back to this), a man came up to me at the end of the church service who had never been to that church before.

"I know that wood plank you were talking about," he told me. "I was the fisherman who stood there before you."

The spot, it turned out, was his favorite fishing hole. He had stood on that wood plank before I ever knew it existed. I got to pray with this man to accept Jesus as his Savior that very morning. This codger of a fisherman gave his heart to Jesus. Yes, the Lord will indeed make us fishers of men!

The reality of my experience at Longview Lake comes down to a few simple words: *All I have ever required of My people is two things: that they believe Me and that they do whatever little thing I have commanded them to do.*

Many of us are waiting for a huge word of commissioning to come, when He has already told us in His Word to love our neighbors or feed the poor right in our own backyards. I have no doubt that as we do something with the power of His presence we have already received, we will get more.

But how many of us receive words as suggestions and not commands? What are the "little" things God has commanded you to do? Did you hear these commands? Does it sound as though the Man Upstairs thinks He is God and has come to rule your life? He has. He has come to take over. The good news is that His will is good. Our little acts of kindness can be a big token of God's love to someone else.

Let's do our little stuff, then, so He can do His big stuff. May a passionate generation of violent, broken, obedient warriors arise and lay hold of the Word of God as the God of His Word lays hold of us.

It Is Time for the Breakers

It is time for the breakers to come forth for this generation. Time to confront the darkness with light. Time for the gatekeepers to open up the way, so that the King of glory will pass before us. It is time for the watchmen on the walls and the kingdom elders at the gates to walk together to prepare for breakthrough for this generation.

The breakers are coming to open the way. A generation of authentic, apostolic men and women, old and young, will walk in these principles and see "the knowledge of the glory of the LORD" cover the earth "as the waters cover the sea" (Habakkuk 2:14).

Right now you might be feeling your heart beat more loudly within you as you read these very lines. "What is this strange thing happening to me?" you may be asking. Your heart is beating in greater harmony with God's as you have pondered the words of this strange book. Do you sense Him drawing near? It is the Holy Spirit calling you to be one of the drums that God, the Chief of all warriors, wants to beat upon. He is calling you to be a breaker. Will you answer the call?

Stop right here. Tell Him that with all that lies within you, you want Him to be honored and glorified. Volunteer to be a watchman on the walls—a prophetic intercessor. This is what you were created for. Offer yourself anew to Christ and His purposes. Don't wait. Tell Him now.

I surrender to the Master and Chief. Consume me with Your Holy Spirit. Take control of my life. Make me into a prophetic intercessor who makes history before Your throne. Put Your breaker anointing upon my life for Your Kingdom's sake. Fill me. Use me. Empower me for Christ's sake. I choose by God's grace to be a watchman on the walls for my family, city, nation and my generation. Like Simeon and Anna, I want to see the purposes of God birthed in my life. Take possession of me, in Jesus' great name. Amen!

Yes, We're Kneeling

Wow! As I composed these last few words, I found myself weeping for you. May these tears fall, in turn, on your heart and undo you with His invitation to make history at His throne.

I am inviting you to continue with me on the journey to be one of those velvet warriors for such a time as this. May you see Jesus and the kindness of His face. And as you do, look through His eyes and see what He sees. Then, for the love of Christ, let this compassion erupt in you until all you can do is serve His purposes through prophetic intercession.

> Kneeling, kneeling,
> Kneeling on the promises of God my Savior;
> Kneeling, kneeling,
> I'm kneeling on the promises of God.

By now you have caught the tune. In fact, I think I just heard you singing with me. May a passionate chorus arise that will change lives and impact nations.

Practical Applications—Making It Real!

- Commit to being a prophetic intercessor that will go before others to change lives and impact nations. Arise and join the ranks.
- Read books on church history and revival. Go visit a historic site where God poured out His presence in times past, and call forth the redigging of that ancient well.

- Visit a location where revival is taking place today—where there seems to be an open heaven or gateway through which His presence is being manifested.
- Meditate and ask what little thing God last commanded you to do. Come before Him with fresh passion to obey.

Recommended Reading

Revival Fire by Wesley L. Duewel (Zondervan, 1995)

The Seer: The Prophetic Power of Visions, Dreams, and Open Heavens by Jim W. Goll (Destiny Image, 2004)

Digging the Wells of Revival: Reclaiming Your Historic Inheritance through Prophetic Intercession by Lou Engle (Revival Press, 1998)

Elijah's Revolution: The Call to Passion and Sacrifice for Radical Change by Jim W. Goll and Lou Engle (Destiny Image, 2002)

21-Day Devotional Guide

T HE FOLLOWING IS a 21-day devotional to accompany *The Prophetic Intercessor*. There are three activities for each day: listen, pray and obey. The "Listen" section contains a passage of the Bible and a related inspirational reading from *The Prophetic Intercessor*. "Pray" includes a suggested prayer based on the theme of the day's reading. The "Obey" portion provides a space for you to record what the Lord speaks to you and to document how He leads you to put your prayers into action. Pray with me as you begin: *Holy Spirit, move upon every area of my life as I listen to You, pray and then obey what I hear You saying to me. For the glory of Jesus and His Kingdom, walk with me as I lay hold of that for which You have laid hold of me. Amen!*

DAY 1 5/23/08

Listen

Abraham said to his young men, "Stay here with the donkey, and I and the lad will go over there; and we will *worship* and return to you."

Genesis 22:5, emphasis added

The first mention of the word *worship* is found in Genesis 22, after the Lord asks Abraham to offer his son Isaac before Him on Mount Moriah. Abraham rises early the next morning, saddles his donkey and launches out in obedience to present his son before God. After three days of travel, Abraham's eyes rest on the site of sacrifice.

We often connect worship with music and sometimes make them synonymous. But there is no mention of music here. The only instruments listed are wood, fire and a knife, and I don't think Abraham had in mind to whittle a flute and play a tune. All he offered was sacrifice, obedience and faith. This is worship in its highest form—a life prostrate before God. Worship is about bending the knee.

Pray

Father God, I realize that my journey as a prophetic intercessor begins with worship. Like Abraham, I humble myself before You. I trust You with all that is precious to me. Only You are worthy of my sacrifice. Only You have the power to resurrect my sacrifice to bear much fruit for Your Kingdom. I worship You by laying my life down before You afresh, right now. I bend my knee to the God of Abraham, Isaac and Jacob and give You the honor that You deserve.

Obey

What I hear You say is "Do you trust Me with your heart?"
I need to stop praying about what I want & start praying about what You want.

200

Day 2   7/17/08

Listen

Whom have I in heaven but You? And besides You, I desire nothing on earth. My flesh and my heart may fail, but God is the strength of my heart and my portion forever.

Psalm 73:25–26

Trust in the Lord with all your heart and do not lean on your own understanding. In all your ways acknowledge Him, and He will make your paths straight.

Proverbs 3:5–6

I have knelt at this clear, winding brook—not on both knees, only on one—and lapped up the water like a dog. Awesome!

What was the Lord searching for that day when He selected three hundred soldiers fit to fight against their strong enemy? He was looking for worshipful watchers. He instructed Gideon to accept only those who lapped the water "as a dog laps" (Judges 7:5). Ever watch a dog eat his food or lap his water? He keeps one eye on the food bowl and the other on whomever is approaching. Ninety-seven hundred of the men who remained dropped quickly to both knees and knelt to quench their thirst. All they could see were their own reflections in the water. But three hundred other soldiers knelt with one knee bent. With hands cupped to their mouths, they were watching to see what was about to appear on the scene—a prophetic picture of worshipful watchers.

Today the Lord is looking for the same. He seeks those on bended knee who are watching and praying, acknowledging that God is the strength of their lives. They are intercessory watchmen on guard against enemy attack.

Pray

*Lord Jesus, no one can compare to You. You are my warrior,
full of strength and power. I look to You for guidance and*

protection. I choose not to lean on my own understanding,
but to look to You in all my ways. You are my Rock and
the strength of my life. Quicken my spirit to be alert
and watchful, to see what You are doing and follow You
wholeheartedly. Give me courage for the battles that lie ahead.
I want to be a part of Your army of worshipful watchers.

Obey

Lord, give me eyes to see, ears to
hear, & a heart to feel what You
are doing. I need You so much!
I am standing on the edge of
something big, huge. I just don't
know what it is or how to
proceede. Come Holy Spirit. Fill me,
guide me,

Day 3

Listen

For it is God who is at work in you, both to will and to work for His good pleasure. Do all things without grumbling or disputing; so that you will prove yourselves to be blameless and innocent, children of God above reproach in the midst of a crooked and perverse generation, among whom you appear as lights in the world, holding fast the word of life, so that in the day of Christ I will have reason to glory because I did not run in vain nor toil in vain.

Philippians 2:13–16

During the roller-coaster ride and the trials, something was imparted to Michal Ann and me. The spirit of prayer and the power of travail were put into our souls. I know for sure that God is faithful and that He answers prayer. I get the awesome opportunity to watch miracles in front of my eyes every day. No one can take that away from me. Our Father God is faithful and He answers prayer.

I want to see the velvet army of God arise. Remember, worship comes before petition. The task of intercession involves reminding God of His Word; taking up the cause of justice in a courtroom hearing; building up the walls to keep the enemy out; and standing in the gap with a cry for mercy, mercy, mercy!

Pray

Father God, I have felt sorry for myself, I have complained and have wanted to quit. But I'm not going to quit. Put Your Spirit of grace and prayer upon me so that I can tenaciously press through every obstacle. You are working in me to desire and to work for what pleases You. Make me blameless in Your sight, without fault in my generation. I want to shine brilliantly with Your glory and hold on to You in every situation. My labor is for You. My life is for You.

Obey

DAY 4

Listen

"May he kiss me with the kisses of his mouth! For your love is better than wine. . . . Draw me after you and let us run together! . . . How beautiful you are, my darling."

Song of Solomon 1:2, 4, 15

I am convinced that the last days battle is a battle of passions. The world flaunts its lustful passions daily without shame. But the Church has often seemed anemic by comparison. It is time for the Bride of Christ to be filled with passion for her Bridegroom and offer extravagant displays of love. What better place to exhibit boundless zeal and holy passion than in the place of prayer? Prayer is the bridal chamber of intimacy with our Husband.

Pray

Jesus, my soul aches to be satisfied. But I have wasted my passions on many empty things. This world has nothing for me. Only You can satisfy me. Stir holy passion within me. I want to be fully alive in You. Draw me to Yourself. I want to run with You. Capture my gaze and provoke my heart to a greater love for You. You are altogether lovely and the delight of my life. Take my breath away.

Obey

DAY 5

Listen

In the same way the Spirit also helps our weakness; for we do not know how to pray as we should, but the Spirit Himself intercedes for us with groanings too deep for words; and He who searches the hearts knows what the mind of the Spirit is, because He intercedes for the saints according to the will of God.

Romans 8:26–27

For three years Jesus did miracles among His people on earth, but for hundreds and even thousands of years, He lives to make intercession. Striking, isn't it? Profound! Startling! I wonder what God is trying to say to us? However you analyze it, Jesus lives for prayer.

May the Father put in us the same relentless, pulsing heartbeat of persistent intercession.

Pray

Holy Spirit, I do not know how to pray as I should. Help me. Thank You for the privilege of entering into the heart of Jesus. Go beyond my thoughts and words and pray through me in whatever way You choose. Release through me effective intercession that expresses Your longings and accomplishes Your will.

Obey I realize that the importance of prayer is the connection & open line of communication between You & I God. Please take my prayers to Your heart. Please give answers Lord. I know that You hear me. I know that You care about the things that I care about. why don't You answer? Why do you seem so silent, so far away? I love You with all of my heart. Come close to me & answer my prayers

DAY 6

Listen

"Shout for joy, O barren one, you who have borne no child; break forth into joyful shouting and cry aloud, you who have not travailed; for the sons of the desolate one will be more numerous than the sons of the married woman," says the LORD. "Enlarge the place of your tent; stretch out the curtains of your dwellings, spare not; lengthen your cords and strengthen your pegs. For you will spread abroad to the right and to the left. And your descendants will possess nations and will resettle the desolate cities."

Isaiah 54:1–3

Perhaps one reason that few wrestle in prayer is that few are prepared for its strenuous demands. This kind of prayer can be physically and spiritually exhausting. You recognize what is at stake: the eternal destiny of an unsaved person, perhaps; the success of an urgent endeavor; the life of a sick individual; the honor of the name of God; the welfare of the Kingdom of God.

Pray

Lord, You are drawing Your Church into greater intimacy with You. Conceive in us what is pleasing in Your sight. Deliver us from our barrenness and release through us the travail that brings forth life. Open the eyes of those who are blind and awaken their hearts to the knowledge of Christ. Make Your Church abundantly fruitful in the nations of the world for Your great name's sake.

Obey

DAY 7

Listen

But Moses said to him, "Are you jealous for my sake? Would that all the LORD's people were prophets, that the LORD would put His Spirit upon them!"

Numbers 11:29

Pursue love, yet desire earnestly spiritual gifts, but especially that you may prophesy.

1 Corinthians 14:1

For this reason I too, having heard of the faith in the Lord Jesus which exists among you and your love for all the saints, do not cease giving thanks for you, while making mention of you in my prayers; that the God of our Lord Jesus Christ, the Father of glory, may give to you a spirit of wisdom and of revelation in the knowledge of Him. I pray that the eyes of your heart may be enlightened, so that you will know what is the hope of His calling, what are the riches of the glory of His inheritance in the saints, and what is the surpassing greatness of His power toward us who believe.

Ephesians 1:15–19

I am convinced that revelatory gifts of God are for the many, not just the few. The Lord is looking for an entire generation of passionate people (called the Church) who will walk in the spirit of wisdom and revelation in the knowledge of the Lord Jesus Christ.

What does it mean to be prophetic or part of a company of prophetic people? God wants each of us to stay so close to His heart that we can speak a relevant word to different areas of society.

Pray

Father of glory, fill me with Your Spirit of wisdom and revelation in the knowledge of Your Son, Jesus. Draw me close to Your heart so I can hear Your heart for those around

*me. Lord Jesus, for the sake of Your great name, release
the gifts of Your Holy Spirit through me. Just as You—the
Word—became flesh and dwelt among the human race, I
want to be Your word in my sphere of influence so others can
see Your glory and Your Kingdom advance in the earth.*

Obey

"Greater things have yet to come.
Greater things are still to be done
in this city." Lord those words are
so true! Show me Your ♡ for the
children & families of Dillsburg. What
do You want me to do? How should
I go about reaching out to them?.
Greater things are yet to be done
in my family. Stir in their ♡'s a
burning desire to return to You. Use
me in any way You see fit. Lord
take my dreams & give them wings!
I know that all things are possible
w/ You. I believe & I receive it all
right now. I will persist in prayer
until You come, so Lord, just
come! You have never given up on
me & I won't give up on You either.
I love You so much. Please come!

DAY 8

Listen

"Now therefore, O sons, listen to me, for blessed are they who keep my ways. Heed instruction and be wise, and do not neglect it. Blessed is the man who *listens* to me, *watching* daily at my gates, *waiting* at my doorposts. For he who finds me finds life and obtains favor from the LORD."

Proverbs 8:32–35, emphasis added

The fast-paced, instant society of our day is diametrically opposed to the gentle, quiet spirits we need to be people of revelation. The Holy Spirit is searching eagerly for those on whose quiet hearts He can write the revelatory words of God.

True prayer involves *selah*. We must pause long enough to quiet ourselves and bend our ears in His direction in order to listen. You cannot hear what another is saying if you are talking all the time. It is impossible! So pause. Wait. Rest. *Slow down.* You will be amazed how this alone will revolutionize your life. And you will find that these ancient keys open those spiritual eyes so that the light of revelation can come in.

Pray

I often find myself in a place of unrest. I am easily
distracted by things of no consequence to Your Kingdom.
Help me to clear my thoughts and quiet my heart. I desire
Your life and Your favor. Train me to listen, watch and wait
so You can write Your revelatory words on my heart.

Obey

DAY 9

Listen

There was a prophetess, Anna the daughter of Phanuel, of the tribe of Asher. She was advanced in years and had lived with her husband seven years after her marriage, and then as a widow to the age of eighty-four. She never left the temple, serving night and day with fastings and prayers. At that very moment she came up and began giving thanks to God, and continued to speak of Him to all those who were looking for the redemption of Jerusalem.

Luke 2:36–38

In what way can <u>Anna</u> be considered a prophetess? The Scripture does not tell us that she wore a coat of camel's hair or ate locusts and wild honey. I doubt that she pointed a long, snarling finger at people and said brazenly, "Thus saith the Lord!" revealing the secret sins of their hearts. We have no clue that she ever confronted the prophets of Baal like Elijah of old or called down fire from heaven. In fact, we find not even one recorded prophecy from this devout woman.

If she did not give personal prophetic words, then what was her prophetic ministry? She was a woman of the secret place, not with a public ministry at all but interceding with the purposes of God for her generation. The expression of her prophetic ministry was her enduring intercession. She was a prophetic, intercessory Jesus fanatic!

Pray

Holy Spirit, I want to be consumed by a vision of the glorious Man, Christ Jesus. Jesus, You are my goal and my prize. I want to be one who listens and watches for Your return. Give me the grace to serve You with fasting and prayer. I call out to You for strength and endurance to be a bright intercessory light all my days, and pass on a passionate torch to those who follow in my footsteps.

Obey

Lord make me a woman like Anna, one after the desire of Your ♥, prophetic intercession.

210

DAY 10

Listen

"For the earth will be filled with the knowledge of the glory of the LORD, as the waters cover the sea."

Habakkuk 2:14

But God . . . raised us up with Him, and seated us with Him in the heavenly places in Christ Jesus.

Ephesians 2:4, 6

The burden of prophetic intercession begins as a flame and grows into a consuming fire as the revelation concerning the purposes of God for our generation increases. It might start as an inner conviction of His will, a sudden awareness of His nearness or hearing of a situation that triggers a spiritual response.

All prophetic intercession carries the struggle of birth. The heart of the intercessor becomes the womb in which God's prophetic purposes come forth. In this place the struggle between old traditions and new ways takes place. We become the handmaidens of the Lord in whom the "new and old wineskins" collide. As we hear God's voice, we become convinced that a radical revolution of the Christian faith is near. The prophetic intercessor conspires with God that His glory will be seen, felt and known in the earth.

Pray

Holy Father, liberate me from my limited point of view. I want to see things from Your heavenly places and join with You to do what is humanly impossible. I embrace the change You want to release in the earth. Let my heart be the womb from which Your prophetic purposes come forth. Give me the tenacity to fulfill my role so the earth is filled with Your glory.

Obey

211

DAY 11

Listen

"Keep watching and praying that you may not enter into temptation; the spirit is willing, but the flesh is weak."

Matthew 26:41

Devote yourselves to prayer, keeping alert in it with an attitude of thanksgiving.

Colossians 4:2

Upon further study, we find that the Bible uses *watch* in two primary ways. One describes a spiritual attitude of alertness in one's heart. The other refers to a specific form of praying. Thus the term *spiritual awakening* often describes what occurs when the Church in a given generation awakens and arises to affect every sphere of society.

We must embrace both meanings and become vigilant in our prayer watching. We must join our works with our faith, go into the world and wake it up with the powerful truth of the Gospel.

Prophetic watchmen can be compared to the night watchmen or security guards of our day. They patrol our cities and guard important places of business while others sleep. They stay awake so that thieves or intruders cannot gain entrance. If a thief does attempt to break in, he will be caught if someone is alert. You see, watchmen are awake on behalf of another.

Watching is to sleeping as fasting is to eating—a sacrifice we make on behalf of another. Watching can also be a weapon of the Holy Spirit in spiritual warfare, and a form of intercession. Watching in the spirit is a powerful tool to bring us into deeper personal communion with our Lord. I love listening, watching and waiting for my Beloved.

Pray

*Father God, help me to watch and pray so I do not enter
into temptation. Strengthen my spirit so that it rises
above the weakness of my flesh. Give me Your grace to
devote myself to prayer, keeping alert with an attitude of
thanksgiving. As I watch and pray, draw me into greater
communion with You, and guard what You have entrusted
to me.*

Obey

DAY 12

Listen

"Therefore keep watch, because you do not know on what day your Lord will come. But understand this: If the owner of the house had known at what time of night the thief was coming, he would have kept watch and would not have let his house be broken into. So you also must be ready, because the Son of Man will come at an hour when you do not expect him."

Matthew 24:42–44, NIV

The Lord is searching for an "Anna Company" in our day, intercessors who will pray through the promises of the Second Coming of our lovely Lord and Messiah. Who will pave the way for the coming of the Lord? New recruits are wanted and the Holy Spirit is sending out invitations today. Have you responded yet?

The real issue, of course, is not whether you are male or female. To be part of this "Anna Company," all you need is an ever-growing conviction of the purposes of God and a desire to pray through God's promises until you see them fulfilled. These revelatory warriors know how to PUSH—*Pray Until Something Happens!*

Pray

Jesus, I want to be ready to meet You. I want to be a passionate Bride, full of power and eagerly watching for You. Wake me and infuse every tired area with Your life. I also ask that You would awaken Your Church so that her lamp is burning brightly with fresh oil. Prepare us to meet You, and help us to prepare others to meet You as well.

Obey

Day 13

Listen

So faith comes from hearing, and hearing by the word of Christ.

Romans 10:17

Have you heard any words from Jesus lately? Just read the red print in the grand Book and let those words sink deep, deep, deep into your spirit. This supplies something for the wind of God to quicken in your heart. Faith will leap up inside of you, and you will have a divine "knowing" (usually the gift of faith). When that happens, you know that you know that you know. You might not know *how* you know—but you are certain everything is going to be all right!

Remember what the Holy Spirit spoke to Michal Ann when she had yielded her right to have children: *I appreciate your attitude, but I am not requiring this of you. I say to you, you must fight for your children.* So fight we did! In fact, one time I came running out of our bedroom after praying and told my wife, "Now Annie, get your gun!"

Recall the words from Isaiah 62:7: "Give [God] no rest until. . . ." So pray *until*! Michal Ann and I prayed until we finally hit the target.

Pray

Jesus, You have the words of eternal life, so I come to You to hear what You want to say. I will treasure Your Word and respond as You instruct. Stir in me greater hunger for Your Word. Help me to feed myself regularly with Your Word so that the Holy Spirit has ample ammunition to move mountains through me. Direct me to hit the right target and accomplish all that I was sent out to do.

Obey

DAY 14

Listen

So I gave my attention to the Lord God to seek Him by prayer and supplications, with fasting, sackcloth and ashes. I prayed to the LORD my God and confessed and said, "Alas, O Lord, the great and awesome God, who keeps His covenant and lovingkindness for those who love Him and keep His commandments, we have sinned, committed iniquity, acted wickedly and rebelled, even turning aside from Your commandments and ordinances. . . . O Lord, hear! O Lord, forgive! O Lord, listen and take action! For Your own sake, O my God, do not delay, because Your city and Your people are called by Your name."

Daniel 9:3–5, 19

Daniel believed the word and declared it as revealed to Jeremiah—that at the end of seventy years of Babylonian captivity, the children of Israel would be released to return to their own land. Daniel also sought the Lord to reveal any obstacles to the prophetic promise being fulfilled (see Daniel 9:3–19). Daniel then responded to the prophetic word by confessing the sin of his people as his own.

The fact that Jeremiah spoke accurately and Daniel later knelt on those words is an example of prophetic intercession at its best. God did precisely what His prophets said He would do! At the end of seventy years the Israelites fulfilled the prophecy of their first return to their covenant land. They began to rebuild the walls of Jerusalem.

Pray

Father God, You are a great and awesome God, who keeps His covenant for those who love Him and keep His commandments. I want to fulfill the prophetic destiny of my generation and remove the obstacles that prevent others from doing so. Give me Your grace to stand in the gap and kneel on Your promises and remind You of Your Word.

Obey

DAY 15

Listen

"Put Me in remembrance, let us argue our case together; state your cause, that you may be proved right."

Isaiah 43:26

On your walls, O Jerusalem, I have appointed watchmen; all day and all night they will never keep silent. You who remind the LORD, take no rest for yourselves; and give Him no rest until He establishes and makes Jerusalem a praise in the earth.

Isaiah 62:6–7

In order to remind God of His Word, we must know it intimately. Get to know your weapon before you use it! This precious Book of promises is as essential to prayer as oxygen and nourishment are to health. Therefore we must be assured absolutely that the Bible is the Word of God.

As we become intimately acquainted with the Word of God, we become intimately acquainted with the God of the Word. Then, as we meditate and pray God's Word back to Him, the Holy Spirit enacts the Word we have just prayed.

Isn't God's plan awesome? Just think: He lets us ask Him to do what He wants to do for us. What a mystery and a privilege!

Pray

Holy Spirit, train me in Your law school. I want to be a successful attorney who pleads cases before the Supreme Court of heaven . . . and wins! Thank You that I can come boldly before Your throne of grace because of the finished work of Christ. Give me a tenacious spirit, one that consistently reminds You of Your Word and gives You no rest until every knee bows and every tongue confesses that You are the Lord.

Obey

Day 16

Listen

Pray for the peace of Jerusalem: "May they prosper who love you. May peace be within your walls, and prosperity within your palaces." For the sake of my brothers and my friends, I will now say, "May peace be within you." For the sake of the house of the LORD our God, I will seek your good.

Psalm 122:6–9

For Zion's sake I will not keep silent, and for Jerusalem's sake I will not keep quiet, until her righteousness goes forth like brightness, and her salvation like a torch that is burning.

Isaiah 62:1

Michal Ann and I now carry a tremendous burden for Israel as prophetic intercessors. Most everything we do on behalf of Israel is connected to one of these three simple activities: proclaiming God's Word, praising His holy name and praying.

Like Elijah I have called for the drought to end and for a time of mercy to begin. I have prayed for the peace of Jerusalem. I have been awakened in the middle of the night just to sit, wait and listen to the voice of God concerning His purposes for the Jewish people. I have been called into active service, alert in the night watches during times of war.

Pray

Father God, give me the Spirit of wisdom and revelation concerning Your prophetic calendar for Israel. Let Your heart for Jerusalem beat in my heart and birth Your purposes through prophetic intercession. Intercede through me until You establish and make Jerusalem a praise in the earth. Cause her righteousness to go forth like brightness, and her salvation like a torch that is burning. Do what You long to do, Lord, for Jesus' sake!

Obey

DAY 17

Listen

But realize this, that in the last days difficult times will come.

2 Timothy 3:1

Thus the Lord GOD showed me, and behold, the Lord GOD was calling to contend with them by fire, and it consumed the great deep and began to consume the farm land. Then I said, "Lord GOD, please stop! How can Jacob stand, for he is small?" The LORD changed His mind about this. "This too shall not be," said the Lord GOD.

Amos 7:4–6

The Holy Spirit is searching once again for a new generation of Daniels, Esthers, Deborahs and Josephs—for such a time as this. He is looking for you. It is time for the grace of crisis intercession to be poured out once again. As the Lord's jealousy draws near, yield!

In fact, I believe His presence is available right now. I have a word for you—"Be possessed by God!" Yes, you can be possessed by the Holy Spirit of God.

This indeed is the key to all effectiveness in life and ministry. This was the key of Jesus, our glorious Messiah, and all the pilgrims of the faith who have followed in His footsteps. And this indeed is the key to crisis intercession.

Pray

Father God, You have granted me authority through prayer. I cry out to You to pardon _____. They deserve Your judgment, but I ask that You relent from Your wrath against their sin. Forgive them, for they don't know what they're doing. Open their eyes to see the mess they're in and cry out for Your salvation. For the sake of Your name and reputation, demonstrate Your kindness and power, and draw them to repentance and faith in Your Son.

Obey

219

DAY 18

Listen

It is time for judgment to begin with the household of God; and if it begins with us first, what will be the outcome for those who do not obey the gospel of God? And if it is with difficulty that the righteous is saved, what will become of the godless man and the sinner? Therefore, those also who suffer according to the will of God shall entrust their souls to a faithful Creator in doing what is right.

1 Peter 4:17–19

Before you go chasing after external dragons and territorial spirits, make sure there is nothing you hold in common with the enemy. Let the finger of God probe into your heart, mind and actions. Open up to conviction concerning your life, family, church or ministry. Repent when necessary. Bring cleansing to your own life through the power of the blood of Jesus and yield to the work of the cross. Destroy the legal basis—the right of the enemy—to attack you. Then you can take authority over the external enemies without receiving the horrendous repercussions of inept spiritual warfare.

Pray

Father, I want to be a person with character strong enough to house the fullness of Your power and gifts working through me. I humble myself before You and yield to the work of the cross. Forgive me for _____. I turn away from my wicked ways and fix my gaze upon You. Release the fear of the Lord into my life in greater measure. I entrust my soul to You, my faithful Creator.

Obey

Day 19

Listen

"Let your heart hold fast my words; keep my commandments and live; acquire wisdom! Acquire understanding! . . . Do not forsake her, and she will guard you; love her, and she will watch over you. The beginning of wisdom is: Acquire wisdom; and with all your acquiring, get understanding. Prize her, and she will exalt you; she will honor you if you embrace her. She will place on your head a garland of grace; she will present you with a crown of beauty."

Proverbs 4:4–9

There seems to be no end to the list of things we need from God. Yet, we must learn to pray for the long haul, rather than just flare up like a Roman candle display. Intense prayers shooting up into the night with a brilliant flash may prompt "oohing" and "aahing," only to fizzle out as quickly as they shot up. If I were given only one thing to ask for, I would follow the example of King Solomon and request wisdom for life's journey. It is the ingredient necessary for the long haul.

Pray

Father God, I ask You for an impartation of Solomon-like wisdom that comes from above. Help me discover what gives life and joyfully embrace all that You have provided for me. Give me the humility to steer clear of criticizing others at all costs. Help me maintain a clean heart, free of bitterness. I forgive _____ for _____. Show me my strengths and help me to use the high weapon of praise effectively in battle. Help me to stick close to the blood. Thank You for the blood of Jesus and its many benefits. Fill my heart with compassion and mercy that I can extend bountifully to others. Show me immediately when I have something in common with the enemy so I can repent and receive Your cleansing.

Capture my gaze so that my eyes remain fixed on Jesus. Give me the discernment to block the counterattack of the enemy. Give me others with whom I can walk on my journey.

Obey

DAY 20

Listen

"The breaker goes up before them; they break out, pass through the gate and go out by it. So their king goes on before them, and the LORD at their head."

Micah 2:13

Oh, that You would rend the heavens and come down, that the mountains might quake at Your presence—as fire kindles the brushwood, as fire causes water to boil—to make Your name known to Your adversaries, that the nations may tremble at Your presence! When You did awesome things which we did not expect, You came down, the mountains quaked at Your presence. For from days of old they have not heard or perceived by ear, nor has the eye seen a God besides You, who acts in behalf of the one who waits for Him.

Isaiah 64:1–4

Truly the Lord Jesus Himself is our breaker—the One who has gone before us and broken open the gates of heaven and hell. He has done it all. But today, as in the days of John the Baptist and other strategic breakers, the Holy Spirit is looking for those who will go ahead of the pack, blaze a trail in the spirit and open the way, that the Lord may "pass through the gate" among them.

Let the breakers arise! Let the breaker anointing be released! Let breakthrough come!

Pray

Father, being a pioneer is painful. Give me strength to continue to break open the way and declare, "Open be the way that the King of glory may come in! Rend the heavens and come down. Make Your name known to Your enemies that the nations may tremble at Your presence!" I ask You for a persevering spirit that seeks until it finds, that knocks until You open the door. Your Kingdom come, Your will be done, on earth in the same way as it is in heaven.

Obey

DAY 21

Listen

"Just as the Father has loved Me, I have also loved you; abide in My love. If you keep My commandments, you will abide in My love; just as I have kept My Father's commandments and abide in His love. These things I have spoken to you so that My joy may be in you, and that your joy may be made full. This is My commandment, that you love one another, just as I have loved you."

John 15:9–12

Many of us are waiting for a huge word of commissioning to come, when He has already told us in His Word to love our neighbors or feed the poor right in our own backyards. I have no doubt that as we do something with the power of His presence we have already received, we will get more.

But how many of us receive words as suggestions and not commands? What are the "little" things God has commanded you to do? Did you hear these commands? Does it sound as though the Man Upstairs thinks He is God and has come to rule your life? He has. He has come to take over. The good news is that His will is good. Our little acts of kindness can be a big token of God's love to someone else.

Let's do our little stuff, then, so He can do His big stuff. May a passionate generation of violent, broken, obedient warriors arise and lay hold of the Word of God as the God of His Word lays hold of us.

Pray

No matter how far I go into the trenches of prophetic intercession, help me to stick to the basics of loving You and loving others. Amen.

Obey

Review the "little things" God has spoken to you during this 21-day devotional. Thank the Lord for the "wins" and take the opportunity to obey Him in areas that require more follow-up.

Notes

Chapter 1 Marching on Our Knees

1. R. Kelso Carter, "Standing on the Promises," *The Methodist Hymnal* (Nashville: Methodist Publishing House, 1964), 221–222.

2. Dick Eastman, *No Easy Road* (Grand Rapids: Chosen, 1971), 123.

3. Joseph L. Garlington, *Worship: The Pattern of Things in Heaven* (Shippensburg, Pa.: Destiny Image, 1997), 5.

4. W. E. Vine, *An Expository Dictionary of New Testament Words* (Old Tappan, N.J.: Revell, 1966), 235.

Chapter 3 Prayer Passion

1. R. A. Torrey, *How to Pray* (Chicago: Moody, 1900), 33–34.

2. Charles G. Finney, *Principles of Prayer* (Minneapolis: Bethany, 1980), 71.

3. E. M. Bounds, *The Necessity of Prayer* (New York: Revell, 1920), 56.

4. William Booth quoted in Eastman, *No Easy Road* (Grand Rapids: Chosen Books, 1971), 92.

5. Stephen Hill, *A Time to Weep* (Foley, Ala.: Together in the Harvest, 1996), 234.

6. Ibid., 240.

7. Ibid., 237.

8. Ibid., 252.

9. Wesley L. Duewel, *Mighty, Prevailing Prayer* (Grand Rapids: Zondervan, 1990), 221–222.

10. Ibid., 222.

11. Ibid.

12. Vine, 182.

Chapter 4 Travail: Birthing the Promise

1. Leonard Ravenhill, *Why Revival Tarries* (Minneapolis: Bethany, 1982), 138.

2. Charles G. Finney, *Lectures on Revival* (Minneapolis: Bethany, 1988), 46.

3. Quoted by Philip E. Howard Jr., *The Life and Diary of David Brainerd* (Chicago: Moody Bible Institute, 1949, 1995), 172–173.

4. Duewel, 210–211.

Chapter 5 Wanted: A Prophetic Generation

1. David Pytches, *Spiritual Gifts in the Local Church* (Minneapolis: Bethany, 1985), 79.

2. Dick Iverson, *The Holy Spirit Today* (Portland: BT Publications, 1976), 155.

3. R. T. Kendall, *The Anointing: Yesterday, Today, Tomorrow* (Lake Mary, Fla.: Charisma House, 2003), 2.

4. Rodney M. Howard-Browne, *The Touch of God* (Louisville: R.H.B.E.A., 1992), vi.

Chapter 6 Watchmen on Guard

1. Rick Joyner, *The Prophetic Ministry* (Charlotte, N.C.: Morningstar, 1997), 199.

2. Ibid., 202.

Chapter 7 Relentless Reminding

1. Jack Deere has written *Surprised by the Power of the Spirit* (Grand Rapids: Zondervan, 1993) and *Surprised by the Voice of God* (Grand Rapids: Zondervan, 1996).

2. Andrew Murray, *With Christ in the School of Prayer* (Springdale, Pa.: Whitaker, 1981), 161–162.

3. This story was told in R. Edward Miller's book *Thy God Reigneth* (Mar del Plata, Argentina: Argentine Bible Assemblies, n.d.). I heard him tell the account

on a video as well. This out-of-print book, according to the jacket, "tells of the beginning of the outflow of God's river of revival to Argentina and its flowing from 1949–1954."

4. Murray, 167.

Chapter 8 Israel: God's Prophetic Calendar

1. Tom Hess, *Let My People Go!* (Washington, D.C.: Progressive Vision, 1987), 118–120.

2. Lance Lambert, *Battle for Israel* (Eastbourne, UK: Kingsway, 1975), 103.

3. Ramon Bennett, *When Day and Night Cease* (Jerusalem: Arm of Salvation, 1992), 122–123.

4. Ibid., 123.

5. Louis Rapoport, "Ethiopian Jewry Rescued," *The Jerusalem Post*, 1 June 1991.

6. Associated Press, "Massive Airlift Transports Ethiopian Jews to Safety," *News Messenger* (Marshall, Tex.), 26 May 1991.

Chapter 9 The Lost Art of Prophetic Intercession

1. Bryn Jones, "Prophetic Intercession in the Final Generation," *U.S.A. PRAY! Training Manual* (Reston, Va.: Intercessors for America, 1989), 43.

2. Andrew Gowers, "American Navy in Second Confrontation," *Financial Times*, 23 September 1987.

3. See Jack Hayford, *Did God Not Spare Nineveh?* (Van Nuys, Calif.: Church On The Way, 1980).

Chapter 10 Crisis Intercession

1. Norman Grubb, *Rees Howells, Intercessor* (Fort Washington, Pa.: Christian Literature Crusade, 1987), 232.

2. Ibid., 234.

3. Ibid., 244.

4. Ibid., 245.

5. Doris M. Ruscoe, *The Intercession of Rees Howells* (Fort Washington, Pa.: Christian Literature Crusade, 1983), 27.

Chapter 11 Wisdom Issues

1. Ken Blue, *The Authority to Heal* (Downers Grove, Ill.: InterVarsity, 1987), 76.

2. Terry Crist, *Interceding against the Powers of Darkness* (Tulsa: Terry Crist Ministries, 1990), 19.

3. Eastman, 61.

Chapter 12 Breakers and Gatekeepers

1. Jim W. Goll, *The Seer* (Shippensburg, Pa.: Destiny Image, 2004), 122.

2. This story is told in chapter 40, "The Revival in the Hebrides Islands," from the book *Revival Fire* by Wesley L. Duewel (Grand Rapids: Zondervan, 1995), 306–318.

Subject Index

Abel, 176
Abraham, 21–22, 124
agonizing, 68–69
Ahab, 71
alertness, 93–94, 95
Amos, 157–60, 165
"Anna Company," 144, 153
Anna (prophetess), 141–44
anointing, 84, 156
anti-Semitism, 136
Argentina, 112–14
armor of God, 182–83

Babylonian captivity, 127–28
Bahrain, 151, 164
Balfour Declaration, 131
barrenness, 30, 37–39, 41, 44, 66–67,
    117–18
Ben-Gurion, David, 124
Bennett, Ramon, 129
Bernard of Clairvaux, 52
Bernis, Jonathan, 133
Bible
    knowledge of, 102
    promises of, 108, 114
    as standard, 107–8

birth struggle, prophetic intercession
    as, 147
blessing, 44
blood, 115, 176–77
Body of Christ, 102
Booth, General, 50–51
Brainerd, David, 63–64
breakers, 185, 188, 196
Bride of Christ, 45
brokenness, 20, 33, 60
Buenos Aires, 113–14

Campbell, Duncan, 188
Campus Crusade for Christ, 34
cancer, 40
Central European Reconciliation Confer-
    ence, 160–61
Central Missouri State University, 34–35,
    36, 41
cessationism, 107–8
Chavda, Mahesh, 41
childbirth, 61–62, 67
Church, 79, 144
    sins of, 161, 164
church growth seminars, 51
church history, 197
Church On The Way, 152

Scripture Index

For More Information

Dr. James (Jim) W. Goll is the cofounder of Encounters Network and Encounters Alliance with his wife, Michal Ann. He is a member of the Harvest International Ministries Apostolic Team and an instructor in the Wagner Leadership Institute, and he serves on numerous national and international councils. He is the author of fifteen study manuals and a contributing writer for *Kairos* magazine, *The Voice of the Prophetic* and other periodicals.

James W. and Michal Ann have four wonderful children and live in the beautiful rolling hills of Franklin, Tennessee.

Books by James W. and Michal Ann Goll include:

The Lost Art of Intercession

Fire on the Altar

The Lost Art of Practicing His Presence

Exodus Cry: Sounding a Prophetic Call to Strategic Prayer for Israel and the Jewish People Worldwide

Elijah's Revolution: The Call to Passion and Sacrifice for Radical Change

The Coming Prophetic Revolution: A Call for Passionate, Consecrated Warriors

Women on the Frontlines: A Call to Courage

Intercession: The Power and Passion to Shape History

A Call to the Secret Place

The Beginner's Guide to Hearing God

The Seer: The Prophetic Power of Visions, Dreams, and Open Heavens

The Seer Daily Devotional Journal

God Encounters: The Prophetic Power of the Supernatural to Change Your Life

Praying for Israel's Destiny: Effective Intercession for God's Purposes in the Middle East

Dream Language: The Prophetic Power of Dreams, Revelations, and the Spirit of Wisdom

Compassion: A Call to Take Action

The Prophetic Intercessor

Angelic Encounters

For more information contact:

Encounters Network
P.O. Box 1653
Franklin, TN 37075

Office phone: (615) 599-5552
Office fax: (615) 599-5554
For orders call: 1-877-200-1604
Email: info@encountersnetwork.com

For more information about conferences, seminars, missions outreach or product resources, or to sign up for monthly email communiqués, visit www.jamesgoll.com or www.encountersnetwork.com.

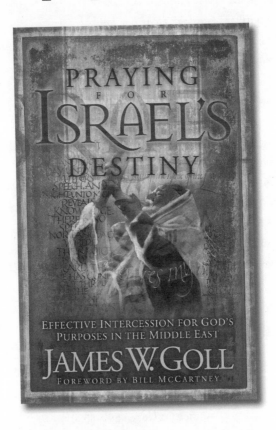